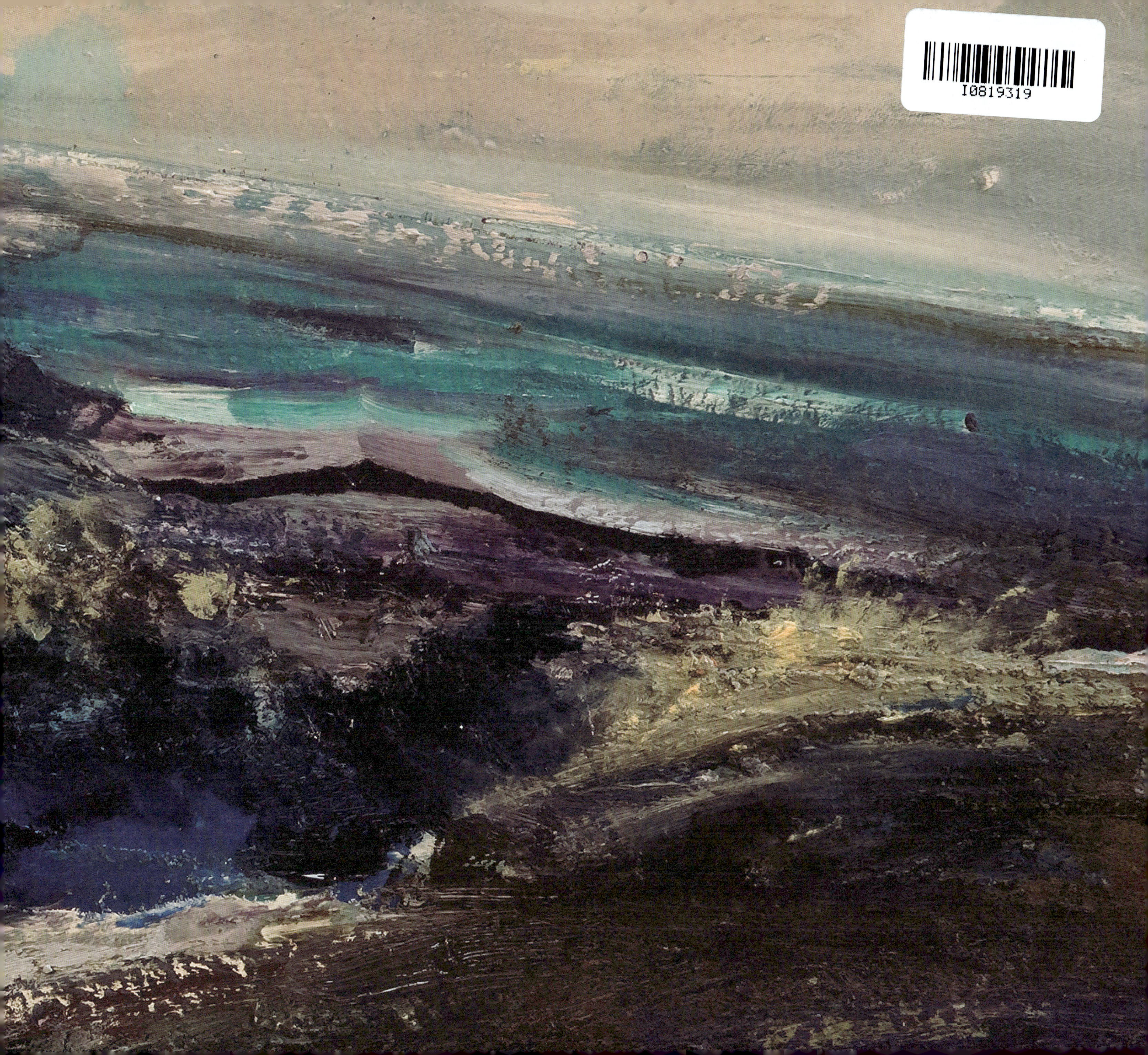

I0819319

Barry Gealt

Embracing Nature

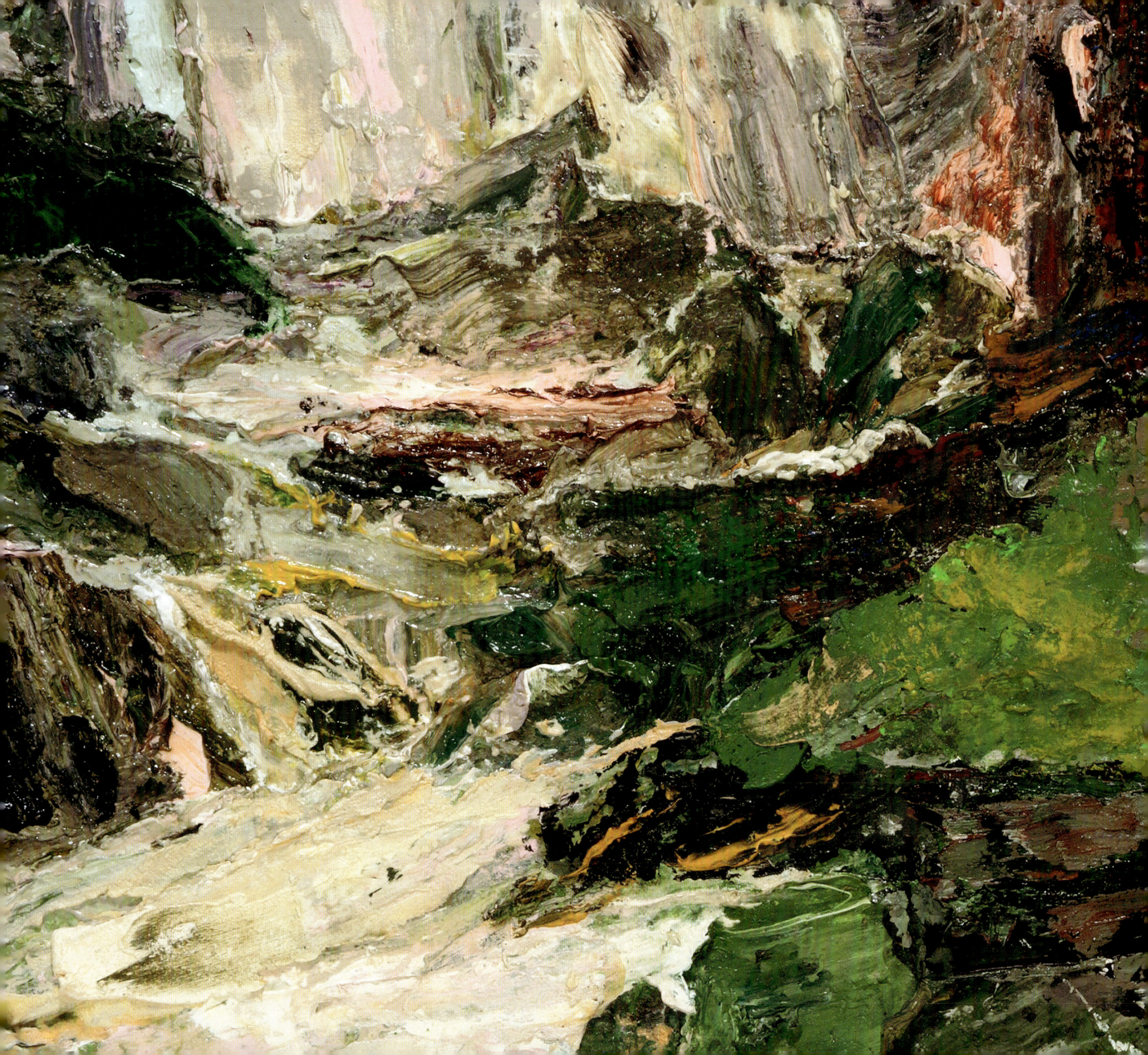

Barry Gealt

Embracing Nature

Landscape Paintings 1988–2012

Essay by

Rachel Berenson Perry

Indiana University Art Museum in association with Indiana University Press, Bloomington and Indianapolis

Indiana University Art Museum, Bloomington
©2012 Indiana University Art Museum
All rights reserved.
All images ©2012 Barry Gealt unless otherwise noted.
This publication, exhibition, and related programming were made possible with support from Anthony Moravec, Lawrence and Lucienne Glaubinger, Glaubinger Foundation, Inc., Ann and Rusty Harrison, Sara and Bob LeBien, Elliot and Chris Lewis, Dorothy and Tim Ellis, Susan Thrasher, Frank and Frances Kelly, Nexus Group, Inc., and Charles Lanham. It is published in conjunction with the special exhibition at the Indiana University Art Museum, *Barry Gealt: Embracing Nature,* October 6–December 23, 2012.

Barry Gealt: Embracing Nature
is distributed by
INDIANA UNIVERSITY PRESS
601 North Morton Street
Bloomington, Indiana 47404-3797
iupress.indiana.edu
Telephone orders: 800-842-6796
Fax orders: 812-855-7931

cover image:
Early September, 5:30 a.m., Oyster Island, Corea, Gulf of Maine, 2009
Oil on panel
22" x 92"
Collection of Jonlee Andrews and Dan Smith, Bloomington
(see also pp. 54–55)

Library of Congress Cataloging-in-Publication Data
Perry, Rachel Berenson.
Barry Gealt : embracing nature : landscape paintings, 1988-2012 / Rachel Berenson Perry.
pages cm
Includes index.
Issued in connection with an exhibition held at the Indiana University Art Museum, fall, 2012.
ISBN 978-0-253-00965-4
1. Gealt, Barry, 1941---Exhibitions. 2. Landscapes in art--Exhibitions. I. Gealt, Barry, 1941- Works. Selections. 2012. II. Indiana University, Bloomington. Art Museum, host institution. III. Title.
ND237.G323A4 2012
759.13--dc23
2012020610

Produced by Indiana University Art Museum Publications, www.artmuseum.iu.edu
Designed by Brian Garvey
Edited by Linda Baden
Photography by Kevin Montague, Michael Cavanagh, and Arthur Liou

Printed by Mossberg & Company Inc.
Printed and bound in the USA.

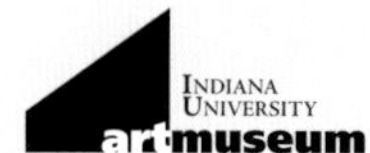

Contents

vi Forewords *Kathleen A. Foster, Michael A. McRobbie*

ix Preface

x Acknowledgments

1 Barry Gealt, A Personal Perspective *Adelheid M. Gealt*

4 Barry Gealt: An Art-Making Life *Rachel Berenson Perry*

23 Catalogue

66 Artist's Chronology

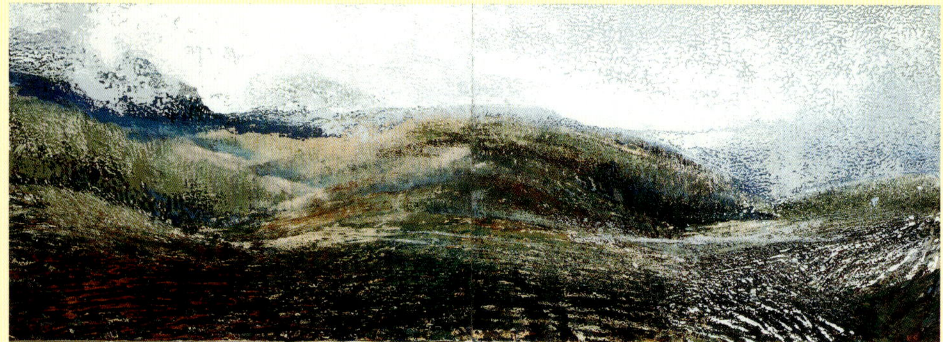

Barry Gealt
Fields of Sweet Owen County, 1994
Woodcut diptych
22″ x 60″
Indiana University Art Museum, 2000.122

Philadelphia, New Haven, Indiana, Normandy: four spots on a life map that I share with Barry Gealt. Since he is a landscape painter, it is not surprising that place has shaped his identity as an artist; I recognize, like familiar geological strata in a roadside cut, the layered experiences of his life as they read out in his art. Barry was born in Philadelphia, where I live now, and he has never lost a certain accent, body language, and tendency to talk very, very fast that I have always credited to his native city. Surely personality has something to do with it, but there is a kind of ebullience in Barry, a boyishness that has been retained from his early years; I'd like to think that his joyous laugh comes straight out of urban Philadelphia.

New Haven, on the other hand, I remember as a serious place. His graduate studies at Yale surely cultivated his intense and thoughtful, ambitious, historically minded self. Perhaps Yale prepared him by exposure to great painters to think of himself in the big game of art history, to believe in the importance of art making, to delve into the pleasures of process. Perhaps, in the company of great teachers, he was inspired to become one, too, a liberal and challenging mentor to generations of students.

Setting down roots in Indiana, he grew. First a figure and then a landscape painter, he found in Owen County a never-ending panorama of natural change, played across sweeping vistas of farmland, and in folded curves of forest and valley. His Indiana landscapes are spectacular: my favorites include his explosive, surging waterfalls, and the monumental woodcut diptych acquired by the Indiana University Art Museum while I was curator there, *Fields of Sweet Owen County,* which gives a powerful sense of the roll of the earth and the eternal movement of the sky. There is poetry in these images, but they are tough and often dark, crusty, mysterious, and grand

New territory opened during a startling first sojourn in France in 2003, when Barry won a visiting professorship at the Terra Foundation's summer residency program for scholars and artists in Giverny. As a member of the Terra's Board of Directors, I nominated Barry for this position, knowing that he was a superb teacher and a collegial soul who would add to the life of the summer community; I also thought he might be tickled by painting in the haunts of the area's most famous resident, Claude Monet. Little did anyone anticipate how Barry would respond to the storied landscape of Normandy. Exhilarated and challenged by the terrain that had inspired so many great painters—Courbet, Whistler, Inness, Monet—Barry brought his own sensibility to views of the cliff-lined, surf-beaten coast. In its feeling for great spaces and natural forces, Barry's Normandy work—like his Indiana landscapes—has a romantic energy, as if Turner's imagination had survived to experience Abstract Expressionism and the tumult of the twentieth century. Like Turner, Inness, and Monet in the last decades of their careers, Gealt arrives at breadth and abstraction after long observation. Composing or reworking from memory, layering and scumbling, he achieves a distilled expression that is both suggestive of nature and also an autonomous artistic event. Atmospheric and appealing to the imagination, the paintings are also sensationally tactile, sculptural in their sense of modeled paint, and so broadly handled that they verge on the non-objective.

Emotion unites the dual experience of these canvases. Thrilling and dramatic, his paintings begin from a landscape that others might see—or represent—as banal or conventionally picturesque. Instead, he reminds us of the sublime and the ancient abiding in the landscape of rural Indiana and France. Recently traveling to new sites on the coasts of Canada and Maine, Barry brings to these new places a mature method along with his innate energy and sensitivity. This force comes entirely from within; geography has little to do with it. The passion of the artist reveals the power of place; place, depicted, reflects the spirit of the painter.

Kathleen A. Foster
The Robert L. McNeil, Jr., Senior Curator of American Art
Director, Center for American Art
Philadelphia Museum of Art

Barry Gealt is an artist of international stature. Over the course of a teaching career that spanned four decades, he had—and continues to have—an enormous influence on countless students who are now practicing artists. Barry's paintings, exhibited in galleries around the world, will long continue to have profound impact even on artists who know him only through his work, and, of course, on art lovers who encounter his beautiful and thought-provoking pieces.

As is the case with all great artists, Barry's paintings change how we see the world. Having found success with his early figurative studies, Barry turned his focus to landscape painting in the mid-1980s. To borrow from the German writer, E.T.A. Hoffman, Barry has "plumbed the deeper meaning of nature" and its images appear on his canvasses "in all their sublimity and splendor." Whether his subject is the coast of Maine, the cliffs of Etretat, or a corner of his Owen County, Indiana, farm, Barry's works are striking for their rich textures and their bold colors. They affect us on a visceral level, but they also compel us to think. They open our eyes and our minds to the potential in nature for order and chaos, its harmonies and dissonances, and, above all, its great beauty.

I am proud personally to own some of Barry's paintings. This exhibition will expose new audiences to his work, and it will solidify his reputation as an outstanding contemporary landscape artist.

Michael A. McRobbie
President, Indiana University

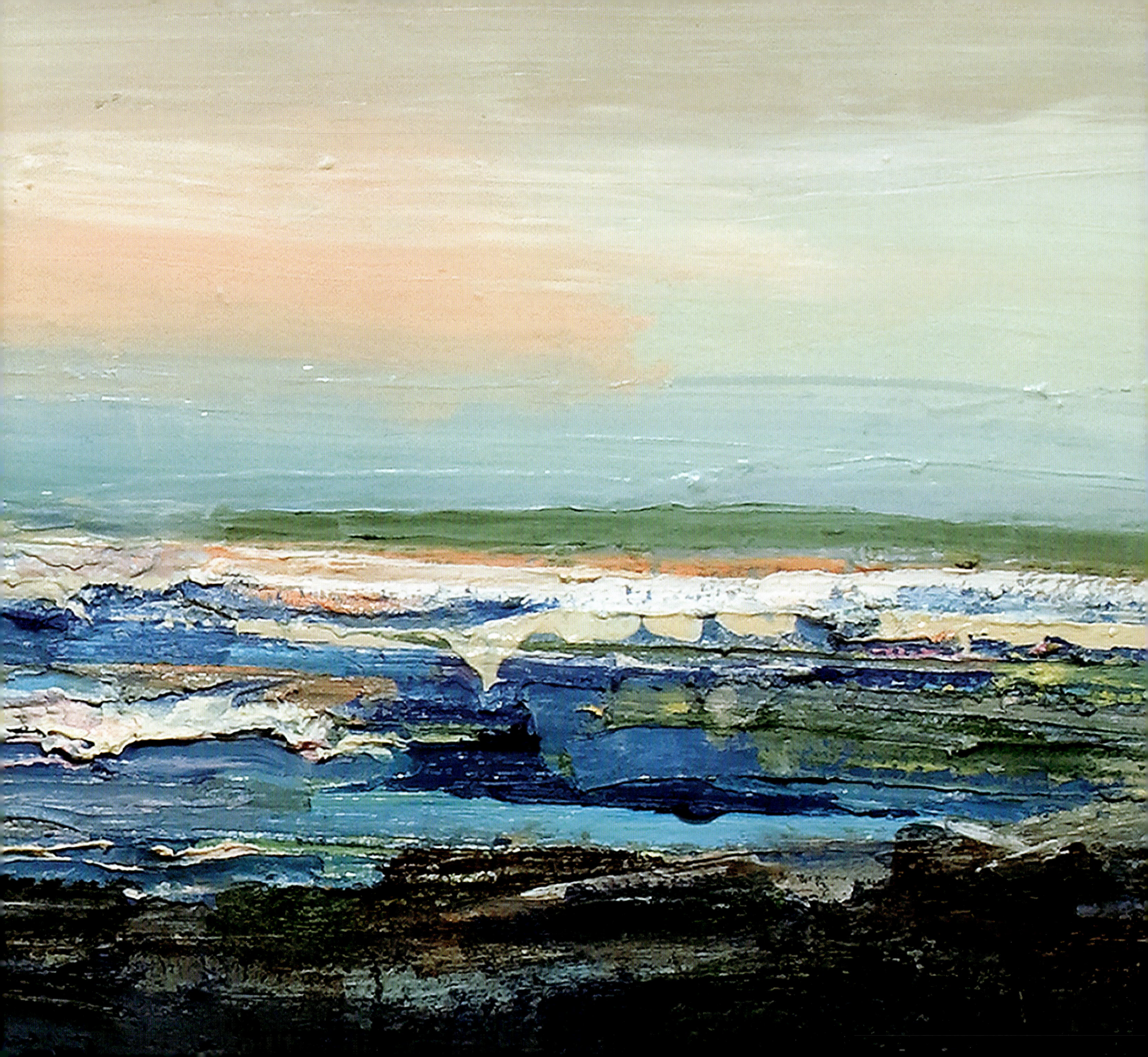

Preface

To view a retrospective of one person's art making provides glimpses into who the artist was at different times, and perhaps one can even see a logical progression of skills and sensibilities to the artist's mature pieces. Art historians love to explore their subject's work to sleuth out influences and make comparisons with identified cultural movements and others' artwork. But to participate in Barry Gealt's bighearted world, one must not be hampered by preconceived notions. Gealt's work, "of his own time," defies categorization.

Despite my usual preference to write about the deceased, I've now learned that writing about a living artist, although confusingly challenging, has the distinct advantage of providing the artist's own professed reasons for creating what he has produced. My heartfelt thanks to Barry Gealt, who, for me, has opened up a whole new way of thinking about art and artists.

Rachel Berenson Perry

Artist's Acknowledgments

Art lives and lives and lives. It has always lived and will continue to live, with imagination and daring. We are alive in an exceptional time of creativity, and I am very proud to be part of it.

I am grateful for this chance to thank the collectors of my work. They have inspired me to create and often to reach beyond the present, to leap forward with new ideas. They have helped immeasurably with their vision and their appreciation of art.

I would like to personally thank the following collectors: Robert and Suzanne Mann, Anthony Moravec, Ann and Rusty Harrison, Gabriele and Dieter Bamberger, Jonlee Andrews and Dan Smith, Rigel Barber, Frances and Frank Kelly, Dorit and Gerald Paul, Lisa and Charles Lanham, Lucie and Larry Glaubinger, Wally Goodman, Dorothy Frapwell, Laurie and Michael McRobbie, Marion Knauf and Thies Knauf, Amanda and Andrea Ciccarelli, Eleanor Earle, and Beth and Fred Cate.

There are many friends that have been important in the sharing of ideas and the exploration of diverse visual thoughts. Thank you to Nancy and Robert Barnes, Kathy Foster, William Itter, Tina Newberry, Caleb Weintraub, Arthur Liou, James Nakagawa, Pamela Parsons, Amanda and Andrea Ciccarelli, Robert Kingsley, Linda Baden, Michael Cavanagh, Rachel Berenson Perry, Nick Hill, Jennifer Moses, Elizabeth Edwards, Sarah and Bob LeBien, Elliot and Chris Lewis, Darla and Michael Hunt, Loris Smith, Kenneth Duling, and Edmund Battersby. And a special thanks to Massimo and Sandro Zecchi, Robert Doak, Jane Potter, Sandra Tokarski, and John Wilson. Their art stores have kept me working with the very best of materials. This book would not have been possible without the skillful photography of Kevin Montague and Arthur Liou and the masterful design of Brian Garvey.

I have always enjoyed the support of my gallery directors. They have tolerated and trusted me when I have had doubts. I never missed our deadlines, but in most of the shows the paintings arrived wet. Many thanks to Mark Ruschman, Telene Eddington, Tina and Knut Osper, Anja Knoess, Lucie Glaubinger, and Jacqueline Stoneberger. And a very special thanks to Stephanie, Trudy, and Rainer Budde.

I have had wonderful teachers who taught me to have an open mind and to respect the field I was entering. Thanks to my mentors, Morris Berd, Bernard Chaet, Lester Johnson, and Jack Tworkov. I would like to thank all my students who have made my life very, very special. You have kept me young at heart and continue to do so.

Rachel Berenson Perry has become a dear friend. We sat down many times as she asked questions that at first I was unwilling to discuss. Her gentle soul and calm persona allowed me to open up. It is never easy to speak of one's self. I refuse to give lectures anymore because I just want the art to speak for itself. She understands the artist's fragile ego and knows how to win your confidence, and she truly listened as I tried to answer her probing questions.

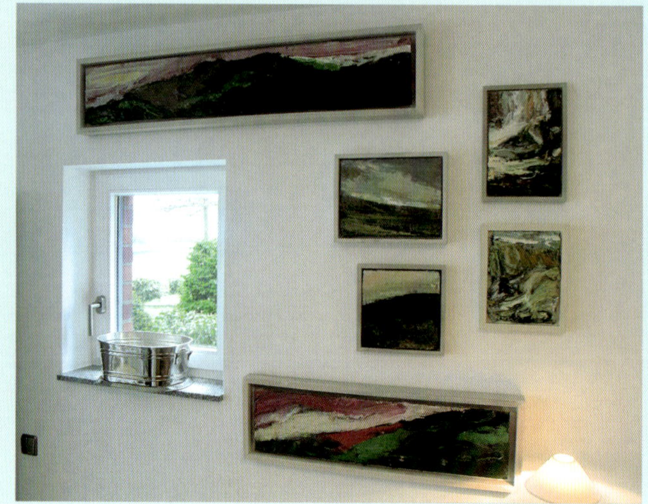

Home of Gabriele and Dieter Bamberger, Cologne, Germany. Photo courtesy Dieter Bamberger

Linda Baden has been my very close friend for forty years. We have conversed on all topics, from family to politics, from art to our love of nature. I can never thank her enough for overseeing this project. She has helped select the works in the show, worked with the collectors, managed the many project details, edited this catalogue, arranged for the special events, and of course has kept me on track. I really owe her a lot. Maybe two lunches a week forever.

A special acknowledgement to my sister Lois and her husband Terre Schott; they have brought great joy to my life.

Now, the best acknowledgement of all, of my wife Heidi, who has encouraged me to be the best person I can be. We have now been together for forty-seven years. We have been married for forty-three years. Without her, none of this would ever have happened. I was from the city and was introduced to nature by Heidi and her family. Her mother bought the farm next to our house, which I have explored and hiked through all the seasons along with the sun, with the morning fog, or the driving rain and the beautiful snow. I absolutely love Heidi's flower gardens. Each year really starts with the blooming of flowering trees and plants that Heidi has nurtured. Our life together has been a continual adventure with mutual passions.

We talk art together, we travel together, we hike together, there isn't very much we don't do together. *I love her with all my heart!*

Barry Gealt

Acknowledgments

Over the course of my career at the IU Art Museum, I've had the pleasure and privilege to work with a number of remarkable artists, from the pioneering metalsmith Alma Eikerman, to the visionary photographer Art Sinsabaugh, to the seminal printmaker Rudy Pozzatti. All shared many of the same traits: boundless creative energy, wisdom, kindness, dedication, and gratitude. No one exemplifies these traits more than Barry Gealt.

Barry makes each encounter an adventure, whether it is going on a road trip to visit a collector, or ordering sushi from the Japanese restaurant on the corner. Always accommodating, never, ever demanding, Barry nevertheless knows what he wants, which he conveys in the nicest possible way. Thus, he makes the perfect partner in a complex project like this, which requires clear vision coupled with a willingness to see others' viewpoints.

As he mentions in his acknowledgements, Barry prefers to let his work speak for itself. But I was privileged to observe the astute author of this book, Rachel Berenson Perry, fine arts curator emeritus at the Indiana State Museum, as she patiently teased the words out of Barry so that she could understand his personal perspective on art, and life. She has done a wonderful job of capturing the essence of the man and his work. Heidi Gealt, the IU Art Museum's director for the past quarter century and Barry's wife of over forty years, wrote a sensitive, insightful introduction to this book, and I am most grateful to her for her willingness to share Barry's world from her intimate perspective. The beautifully written Forewords by Kathleen A. Foster and President Michael A. McRobbie added just the right grace notes to the book.

My "day job" is as head of publications at the Art Museum, so wearing a new hat as curator of *Barry Gealt: Embracing Nature* was a challenge made infinitely easier by the graciousness of my colleagues at the IU Art Museum. Our head curator Diane Pelrine and curators Jenny McComas, Nan Brewer, and Judy Stubbs have been generous with their expertise and suggestions, as has Rachel Perry. Anita Bracalente, the museum's registrar, kept the nuts-and-bolts side of the project on the straight and narrow, and our gallery technicians, Max Shaw and Dennis Deckard, were always willing and more than able to accommodate our installation needs. Aleah Holland, the Art Museum's editorial graduate assistant for 2012, helped with all aspects of the publication. Thanks go as well to Katherine Paschal, the Art Museum's marketing coordinator; Carol Dell, associate director for administration; Paul Sturm, associate director for development; and Anita DeCastro and Ann Fields, special events coordinators.

My partners at the IU Art Museum, Brian Garvey, the museum's art director, and Kevin Montague, head photographer, were unfailingly supportive throughout this project. Brian Garvey designed this beautiful publication, which is illustrated with many images of Barry's work taken over the years by Kevin and the late Michael Cavanagh, as well as by the artist Arthur Liou, Barry's colleague in the Hope School of Fine Arts. Brian also gave invaluable feedback on the design of the exhibition. Kevin provided succinct, pithy advice on the project as we traveled the state, taking digital photos of many of the newer works in private collections.

The Art Museum is very grateful to the lighting designer and IU theatre department faculty member Rob Shakespeare, who offered his world-class knowledge and skills to the exhibition. Professor Shakespeare created the specifications for the new LED lights that were used by the museum for the first time in the Gealt exhibition, and he also designed the lighting of the show itself. Janet Rabinowitch, director of IU Press, was unfailingly helpful with the publication, and we were honored to work with her on this project.

To the donors who made this publication and exhibition possible, we extend our deepest gratitude. Anthony Moravec, chairman of the IU Art Museum National Advisory Board, and a collector with a fabulous eye and a big heart, was more than generous with his time and financial support. Lawrence and Lucienne Glaubinger, the Glaubinger Foundation, Inc., Ann and Rusty Harrison, Sara and Bob LeBien, Elliot and Chris Lewis, Dorothy and Tim Ellis, Susan Thrasher, Frank and Frances Kelly, Nexus Group, Inc., and Charles Lanham also were generous in their support of this publication and exhibition, and we thank them sincerely.

And finally, we offer our sincere thanks to the lenders to the exhibition for sharing their beloved Gealt paintings with us all.

Linda Baden
Curator, *Barry Gealt: Embracing Nature*

I am so pleased to add my deepest thanks to the notes of gratitude expressed by Barry and Linda Baden. This is a project that was obviously very close to my heart, and I am immensely thankful for all the care and effort taken by everyone involved. I add my special thanks to IU President Michael McRobbie, who so generously agreed to write a foreword to the publication, and to our donors and lenders, who made this publication and exhibition possible.

Adelheid M. Gealt
Director, Indiana University Art Museum

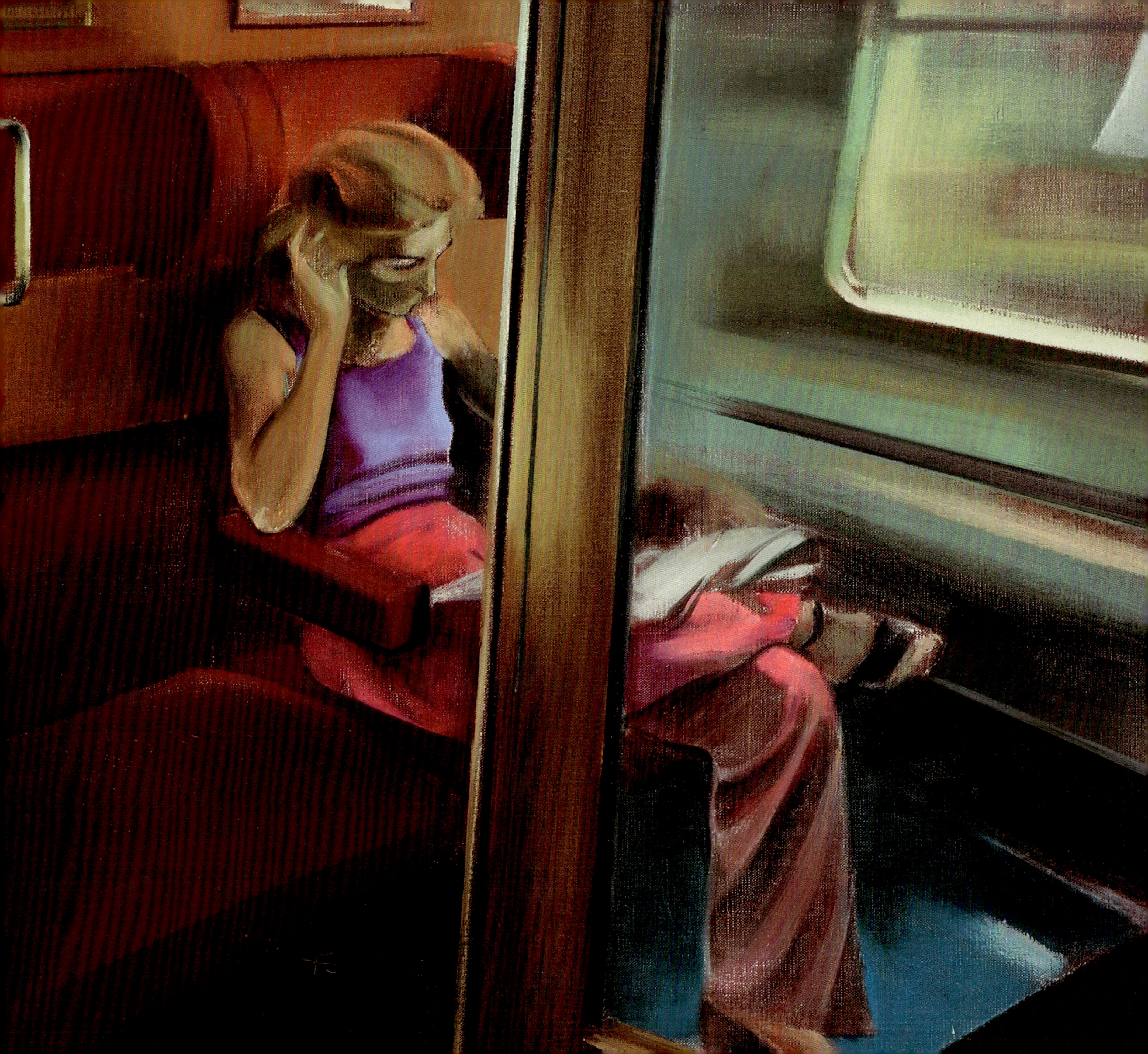

Barry Gealt, A Personal Perspective

Adelheid M. Gealt

In writing about the artist Barry Gealt, who happens to be my husband, I am naturally biased. It is my privilege to have been an eyewitness to his creative process since we met in 1965 and especially since our marriage on the Ides of March 1969. From then on, I was usually the first person besides Barry to see what was happening inside his studio. Once he moved from his IU studio on the third floor of the Fine Arts building (it had been formerly occupied by distinguished artist Harry Engel) to the studio at our home in Spencer that he built in 1987, Barry's art-making process, his joys, his frustrations, his failures and his successes, were something I experienced every day. Knowing when a painting "worked" was a visceral feeling, far beyond critical analysis. I would experience the same rush of joy that came from seeing the treasures in any museum. My response to his work was not manufactured. The hard part was Barry's sensitivity to my reaction. He could tell when his work thrilled me, and he could tell when I was merely being polite.

When Barry and I met in 1965 he had recently established the art department at Wright State University in Dayton, Ohio, where I was then enrolled as an undergraduate. Barry stood out in that conservative Midwestern environment. He wore colorful ties and drove a Jaguar (when it ran). On our first date I drove him to his Jaguar repair place. His most profound quality then, as it is now, is Barry's sensitive response to the natural world around him. He was enchanted by the menagerie my parents kept. He befriended nearly all the creatures that came his way, and he invariably responded with similar joy to the bountiful beauty that nature shares with those who take the time to see it. Whether it was seeing the moon sliding out from behind a cloud, or the flush of delicate color as the sun went down, Barry and I have always shared the pleasure of these fleeting moments.

After a lengthy courtship, we married on March 15, 1969, at a modest ceremony attended by eleven friends at the Quaker church in Xenia, Ohio. By September of that year we had moved to Bloomington, where Barry had accepted a position and I had entered the graduate art history program.

Our first home was a little farmhouse on Schacht Road, off Henderson Street. That first day Barry feared he would be stampeded by the herd of cows in the adjoining pasture. Over time we befriended the local bull who appreciated the aprons full of apples we gave him at summer's end. Our kitchen faced westward down a hill. Evenings were spent in the kitchen watching the sun set. By 1973 we moved to eight acres north of Spencer in Owen County, the home we have treasured to this day. We lost the sunsets but gained a view of a beautiful valley flanked by trees, intersected by streams with several waterfalls at the edge of the woods. Barry's first day of exploration brought him nose to nose with a fox, when, out of curiosity, he stuck his head into a cave near the waterfall. Since then, we've seen foxes, turkeys, deer, coyotes, all sorts of frogs, toads, snakes, and birds and have never lost our pleasure in nature's changing moods over the times of day and successive seasons.

What has inspired Barry to create, I believe, is a fundamental drive to give meaning to existence. Major traumas, both personal and historic, have shaped his understanding of life. In the first half of his creative career, the figure was the subject through which he gave life meaning. During the second half landscape has been his subject. In either case, history, both universal and very personal, is an underlying theme. While he was in college, his closest cousin, Beverly Samans, was murdered in Boston. This tragedy not only permanently affected his family, it also reinforced Barry's determination to give his own and his cousin's life greater meaning. Human beings and human relationships shaped Barry's subject matter in those years, as did the standard subjects artists tackled: still-life and the nude. I still remember many visits to Barry's IU studio, where among the jumble of still-life objects, chairs, carpets, and his pet parrot (who used to sit on his shoulder and chew up his collars as he worked), there would be still-lives and nudes, painted and drawn, in various states of completion. One of my favorites was a grouping of horseshoe crabs, whose shells we had collected on a New Jersey beach one summer.

Once he was ensconced in his large, quiet studio in Spencer, Barry gradually changed first his subjects and later his choice of materials. From depictions of figures posed in a space, Barry expanded to explore scenes of people in action. He did studies of me on the train (during my research trips to Italy); he was fascinated by everyday activities—a friend in a phone booth, the act of brushing one's hair. This evolved into a series of works devoted to dinner parties with friends and family. Barry created a wonderful suite of drawings which captured the distinctive characteristics, gestures, expressions, and attitudes of people he knew well, such as colleague Bob Barnes puffing away on a cigar, attorney Dorothy Frapwell tenting her fingers as she made a funny but effective point in conversation, or my brother Rudy's wild hair.

By the time Barry made those drawings, the beauty of our environs in Owen County had begun to cast its spell. Barry's first forays into the natural world involved drawings. He once woke me to tell me excitedly that he had just drawn a tornado! The morning fog so characteristic of Indiana heat captured his imagination, and he began a magical series of drawings that evoked fog, sun, clouds, and the like.

He was fascinated by our waterfall, a regular destination on our walks. He liked the power it reflected, the fact that trees and stones were in a jumble, that nature was both destructive and ever regenerative. He painted the waterfall many

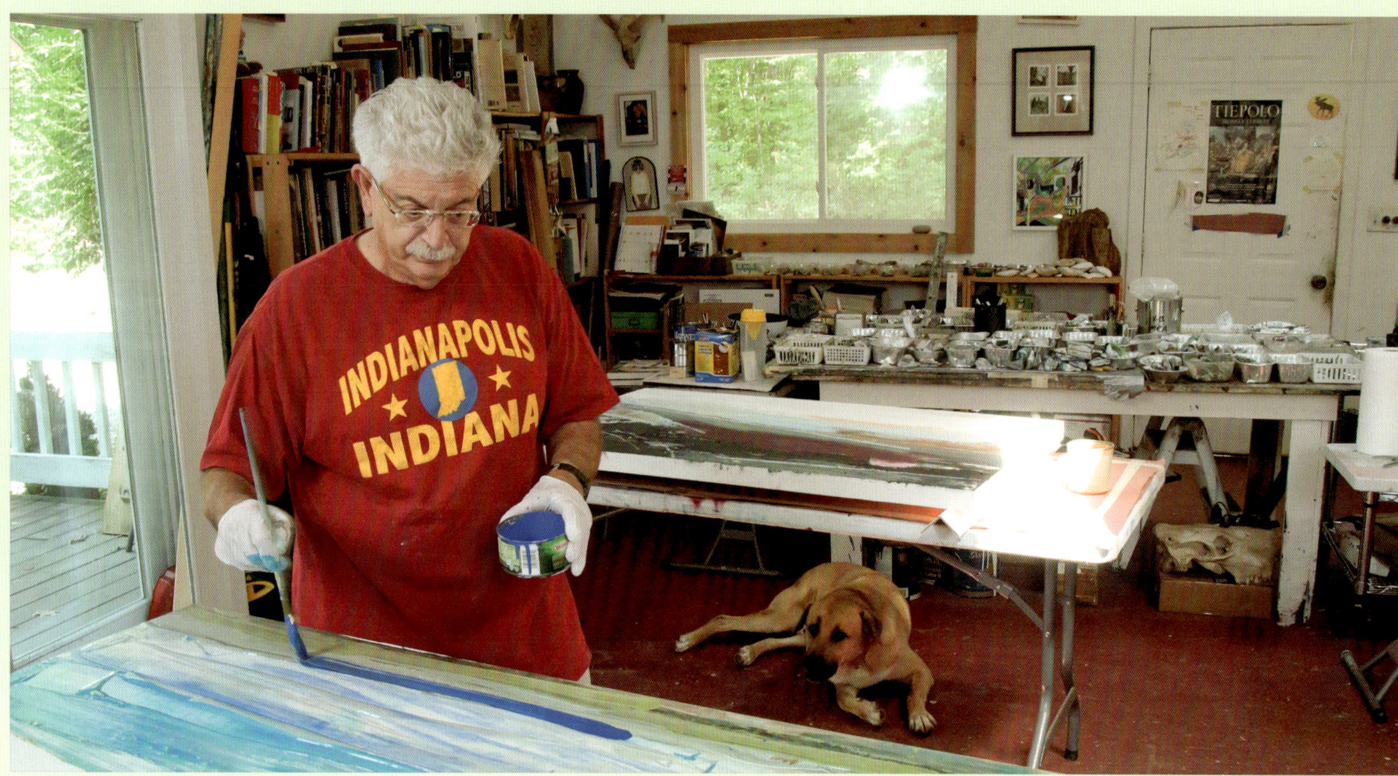

Barry Gealt in his studio in Spencer, Indiana, 2012

times, often in moody nocturnal states that emphasized nature's raw power. The product of an artistic education that emphasized process, Barry became immersed in that elusive world where painting encompassed paint, image, process—an impossible juggling act which left him often downcast, frustrated, and unwilling to let me see his work. He knew me too well to doubt my reaction and so only let me see things when he felt they were done. Often I shared his frustration, feeling that the canvas had been worked too hard, stifling the space, air, and vivacity that these images had possessed at the outset.

Barry turned to a different material at that time, as he began to explore the potential of that most raw and basic medium: the woodcut. He experimented with several different kinds of wood, finally finding some that suited him. He scoured hardware stores, antique shops, and art supply stores for carving tools. He chipped and cut and printed ceaselessly. Instead of a single printing, he overlaid block after pigment-laded block. Barry's woodcuts looked more like paintings than like prints.

All of his woodcuts explored natural themes. His vision was enriched by a trip to China and Japan in 1992/93 to study workshops, supported by the Lilly Endowment. He visited both carvers and printmakers and bought all sorts of new tools. Barry's work with woodcuts was a transformative period. He mastered a difficult and demanding medium. His engagement with this material led him to a different mastery of paint as well.

Barry's interest in landscape continued to expand. His subjects ranged from our familiar forests and valleys and waterfalls to other places that artists' favored or that were important historically. In 2005 we made a trip to Normandy where we visited the cemeteries with their ordered crosses and endless rows of markers and the bunkers still to be seen along the bluffs overlooking the sea. Barry responded to both the historic and the artistic heritage that Normandy represented. Walking the cliffs at Etretat, I remember Barry being riveted by the sight of seagulls, chalk cliffs, and sea witnessed from wild angles and crazy heights, as we were continuously buffeted by the high winds. As soon as he returned to his studio, Barry painted his own paean to this vivid and important experience. The paintings flowed easily with no struggle. Now he was painting with such power and such immediacy, as if the combined hands and vision of all the historic painters who had also painted Etretat animated him as he created that magical breathtaking body of work! My deeply felt response was and remains profound admiration.

A later visit to Brittany added another dimension to Barry's response to nature. The huge granite rocks forming the barrier between sea and land were coated with lichens—many of them a curious and fascinating mustard yellow. Barry was captivated by those rocks, their lichens, and their relationship to the sea on one side, the land on the other. A marvelous series of paintings ensued, many of them experimenting with relief, which form an especially beautiful period of his work. Most of these paintings/sculptures—reflecting the rugged coming together of rock, sea, earth, and sky—are in various private collections. But one of my greatest treasures is the painting Barry made especially for me, which now hangs in our bedroom and which I admire every day.

In recent years, Barry's quest for places that offer distinctive experiences of rock, sea, sky, and land has taken us to Maine, New Brunswick, and Prince Edward Island, and the quest continues.

For several summers we have spent a week in Corea, Maine, in a spot just feet from the ocean where giant granite boulders separate land from ocean. There we have witnessed storms and sunshine, morning glow and evening shadows. There the continual flow of waves, sometimes lapping, sometimes crashing against the rocks, has sustained his interest. At the same time, our great old waterfall at home in Spencer remains a favorite subject as well. He visits it regularly as he makes his rounds of places (some familiar and local, others far away and newly fascinating) where the elements combine to provide subjects for his work.

Most often his materials are now panels on which he can place his paintings in all the different ways necessary to create the effects he desires. He pours, he gouges, he paints, he uses the back of the brush, he uses palette knives, his fingers, and sometimes his whole hand. He still struggles, juggles, revises—but he also has a great sense of confidence, of knowing what he wants and what the painting requires for it to be successful in his eyes. After years of effort, he has (although

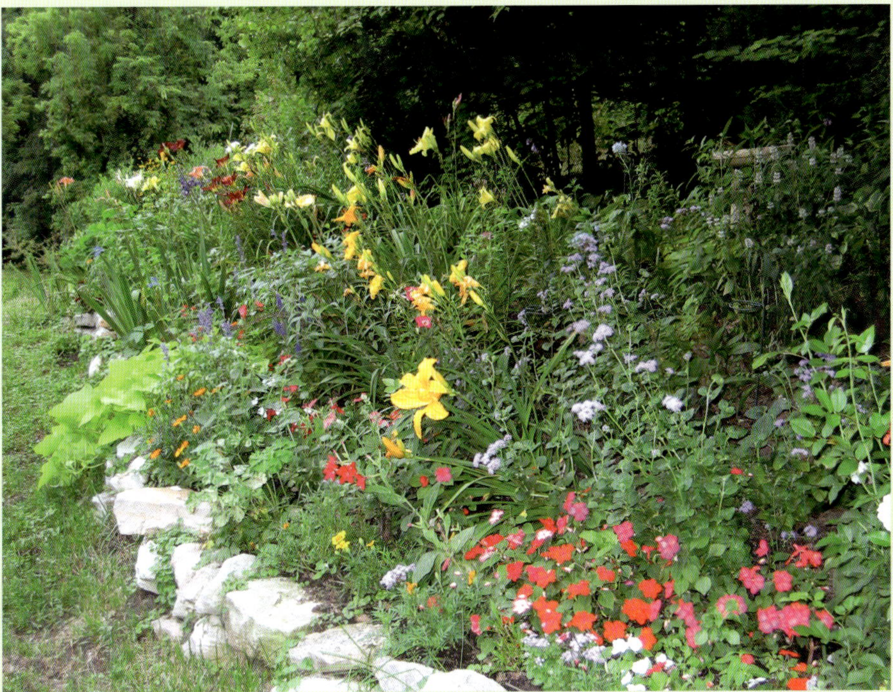

One of the gardens at the Gealt home in Spencer.

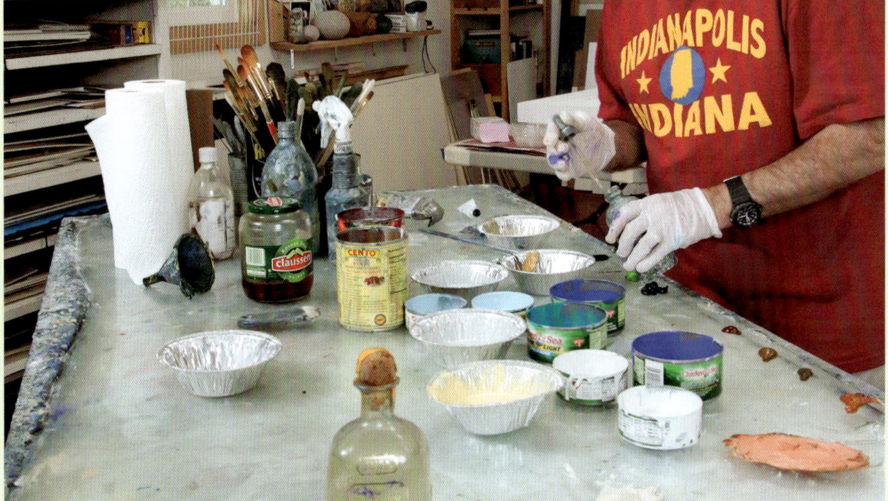

he would never say it) a sense of mastery—over his materials and over his subject. He knows where to find what interests him and how to make his materials reflect his vision. As he has matured and become a master artist, he continues to paint with passion, enthusiasm, and a sense of the quest. The spiritual dimension to his work, which is something he reticently acknowledges, has been an inspiration to other artists over the years.

Through it all Barry has remained intensely modest. He doesn't boast and never belittles anyone else's work, as he takes pleasure in his own accomplishments. What I appreciate most about Barry now is his unflagging devotion to his art, to the natural world, and to the creatures that come our way. Barry has never lost his love for or appreciation of what we are privileged to see every day. Whether it is moonlight shining through the trees or the pale texture of hoarfrost coating the world in white of an early morning, Barry savors what nature offers to us.

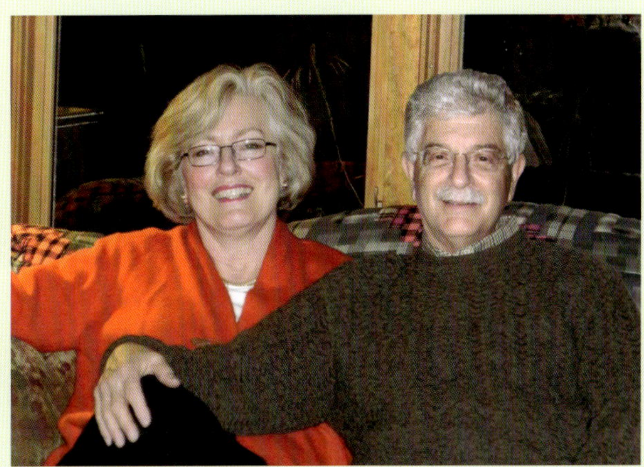

Heidi and Barry Gealt at home in Spencer, 2011.

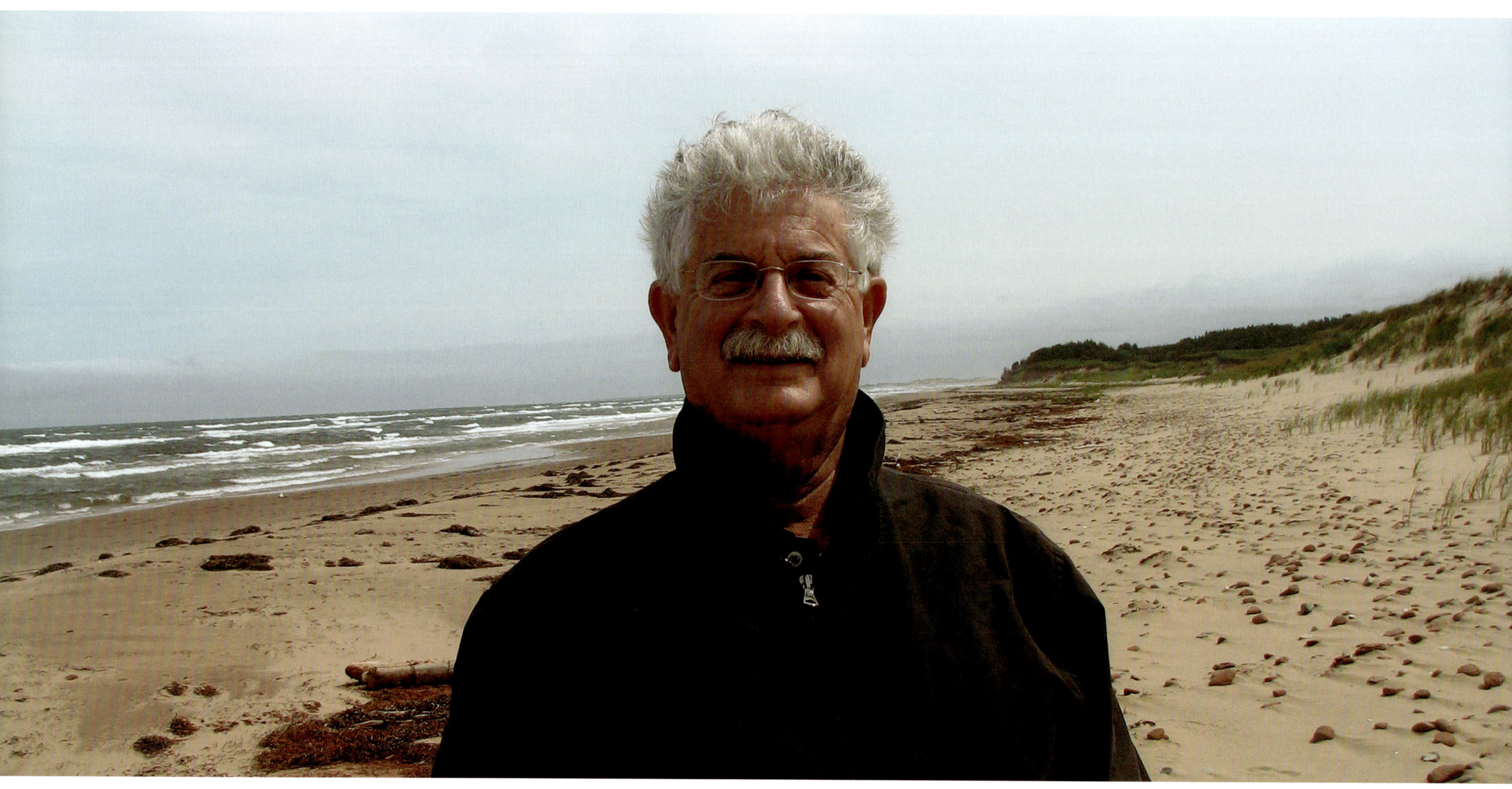

Barry Gealt

An Art-Making Life

Rachel Berenson Perry

"Others plan who they want to be. I just want to paint."

——Barry Gealt, October 20, 2011

The Formative Years

Barry Gealt's paintings elbow their way into your consciousness. Glistening cavern walls reflecting filtered daylight; gushing spring cascades; hump-backed hills looming out of morning fog; surging ocean waves—all conspire to transform you from observer to participant. No amount of viewing on line or leafing through catalogues can prepare you for meeting these paintings face to face, whether in a well-appointed home or in a gallery exhibit. Like photographs of sculptures, reproductions of Gealt's paintings are merely suggestions. In person, his molten, roiling layers of pigment and saturated colors demand your undivided attention.

Like the man himself, these paintings are bursting with life. Barry Gealt (b. 1941) grew up in Philadelphia, where his uncle, Harry Benn, recognized his interest in art and enrolled the seven-year-old in weekend classes at the Fleisher Art Memorial, a school offering free art instruction. His parents, Sylvia Benn Gealt (1917–1999) and Leonard Gealt (1911–2003), both second-generation Americans of Eastern European Jewish ancestry, raised their two children, Barry and Lois (b. 1945) on Leonard's truck-driving salary from the American Oil Company (later AMOCO). Gealt remembers, "As a kid, I grew up in an old world immigrant area with trolleys, markets, a fish store. I loved sports, but always went to art school on Saturdays."[1]

Beginning at age ten, along with two other youngsters, Gealt studied with sculptor Gerd Utescher (1912–1983) for seven years. They saw works in progress: sculpted figures, bas-reliefs, large textured ceramic vessels. They learned how to make things: pinching clay, carving wood, chiseling stone. There were no academic terms, no art history lessons. Their creations sufficed in themselves.

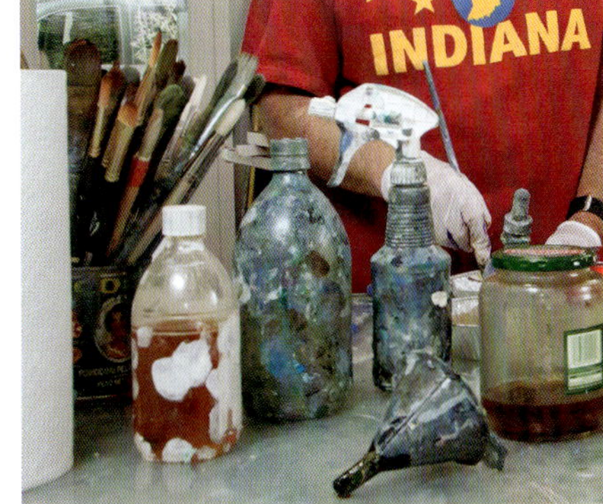

After high school, although Gealt professed his desire to become an architect, his wise mother suggested fine art. Enrolled in the Philadelphia College of Art from 1959 to 1963, under the tutelage of the painter Morris Berd, Gealt explored various mediums and concluded that he wanted to be a painter. He'd admired Winslow Homer's (1863–1910) watercolor seascapes and wanted to create representational paintings. But art schools at that time were influenced by the emergence of Abstract Expressionism, Pop Art, and hard-edge painting, styles which rejected realistic imagery and emphasized abstract ideas. Gealt's professors dismissed Winslow Homer as a mere illustrator who drew pictures for commercial advertisements, and they encouraged him to experiment with abstraction.

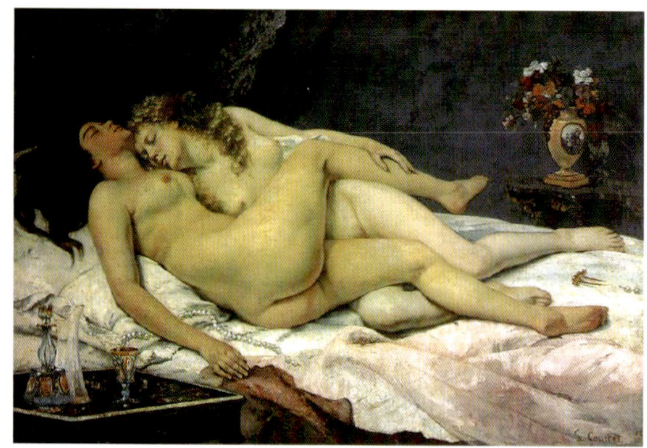

Fig. 1
Gustave Courbet (French, 1819–1877)
Sleep, 1866
Oil on canvas
Petit Palais, Musée des Beaux-Arts de la Ville de Paris

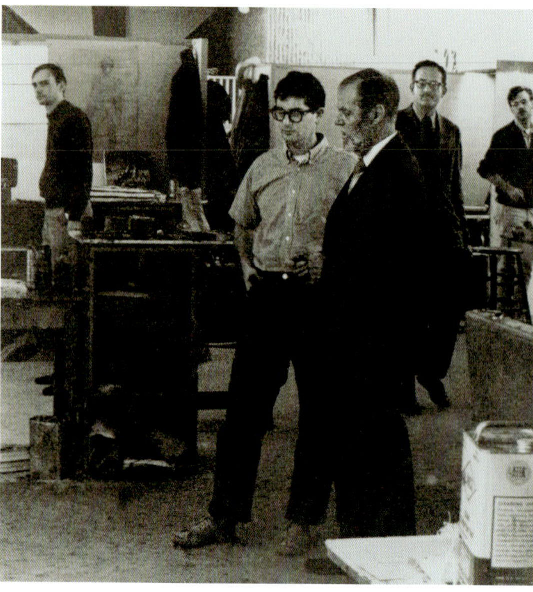

Fig. 2
Barry Gealt with Edwin Dickinson and Bernard Chaet at Yale, 1964
Photograph, collection of the artist

A major exhibit of large figurative paintings by Gustave Courbet, organized by Henri Marceau at the Philadelphia Museum of Art, arrived in town in mid-December of 1959. Gealt noticed a crowd around one painting—some viewers staring incredulously, mothers pulling their children away—and he marveled that the painting, *Sleep* (1866), of two intertwined nude women, retained the power to cause a commotion almost a century after its creation (fig. 1). The strong public reaction to this work infused Gealt with a sense of the magnificence of art: its capacity to stir intense emotions and beliefs; its significance in society. This perception, of the importance of art, stayed with him. It became the guiding principle in his work and his life.

Accepted to graduate school in studio art at Yale University in 1964, Gealt entered a program that emphasized both painting from observation and the exploration of abstraction. Landscape painter and watercolorist Bernard Chaet (b. 1924), and Abstract Expressionists Jack Tworkov (1900–1982) and Lester Frederick Johnson (1919–2010) were his principal instructors. Gealt's work struck a chord with the important American painter, Edwin Dickinson (1891–1978), who visited Yale in 1964 to critique students' work (fig. 2).

In the early 1960s, great social upheaval disrupted America's college campuses. Race riots sparked by the killing of civil-rights activist Medgar Evers and the assassination of President John F. Kennedy plunged the nation into unsettled times and deeply affected Gealt. Jose Clemente Orozco's murals about the Mexican Revolution—and in particular the painting titled *Combat* (1927, fig. 3)—portrayed disturbing images of undulating headless fighters that influenced Gealt's visual responses to America's turmoil. Expressing his reactions to the pervasive unrest brought a newfound authenticity to his paintings. He later remarked, "How to find your individual voice in making 'real art?' Tragedy may be important. For great art, you must find something to speak about."[2]

Jack Tworkov selected Gealt for his handpicked second-year class. After spending the intervening summer at the Yale-Norfolk Summer Painting Program producing "pretty pictures" in a French mode inspired by the work of Paul Cézanne (1839–1906) and Edgar Degas (1834–1917), Barry invited his instructor to view his new

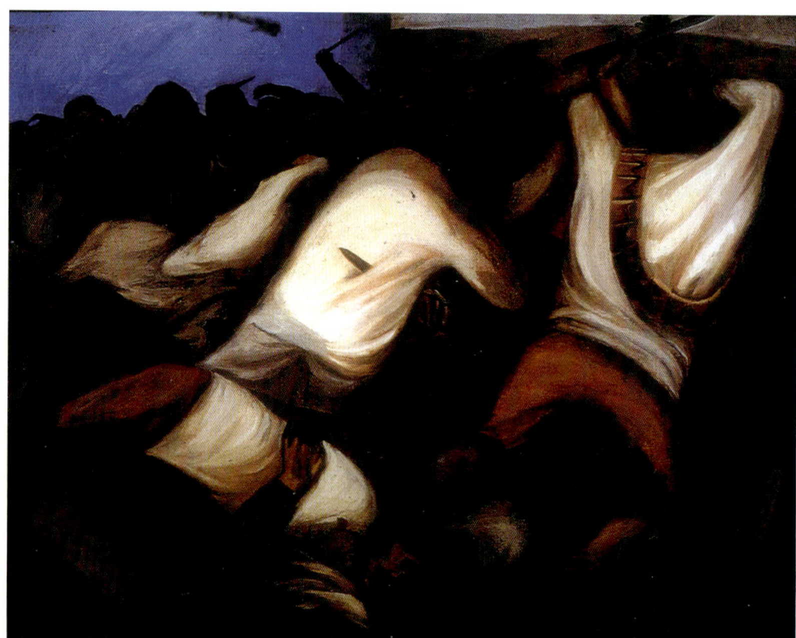

Fig. 3
Jose Clemente Orozco (Mexican, 1883–1949)
Combat, 1927
Oil on canvas
Museo de Arte Carillo Gil, Mexico City, Mexico
© 2012 Artist Rights Society (ARS) / SOMAAP, Mexico City

work. “I didn’t choose you to paint like this,” Tworkov growled in disgust.[3] “As soon as Tworkov said that to me, I totally understood and agreed,” Gealt wrote. “I had stepped backward [in time], and [I] tried to exit that mode of thinking as soon as possible. But I understood that I was searching for something. I really wanted my work to be of my own time.”[4]

Immediately following graduate school, Gealt accepted a job at Wright State University in Dayton, Ohio. During his tenure from 1965 to 1969, he founded and built their art department, while devoting his free time to his own work. “I didn’t do anything that would get in the way of being an artist,”[5] he said. This unswerving commitment to “being an artist”—that is, to making art despite all the other pressures of life—continues to define him.

There was one diversion, however. He met and fell in love with Adelheid (Heidi) Medicus, a chemistry student who had emigrated with her family from Germany to the Wright-Patterson Air Force base near Dayton, Ohio, in 1950, where Heidi’s inventor-father was employed. Her parents opposed the relationship, and the couple chose to elope in 1969. Indiana University’s Hope School of Fine Arts (then called the Fine Arts department) offered Gealt a job as an assistant professor of painting that same year, and he and Heidi relocated to Bloomington.

His early years in Bloomington saw Gealt grapple with the desire to paint past the decorative; to make work that was vital. A series of large, representational still-life paintings of cacti, which he worked on in the mid-1970s, presented a mundane subject at a monumental scale (fig. 4). Moving on from the series of still-lifes, Gealt turned to images of his wife, captured during fleeting, intimate moments at home. These contemporary versions of “genre” paintings, compellingly present, resonated with viewers. In 1984 Hollins University in Virginia mounted an exhibition that included Gealt’s large painting of a nude reflected in a full-length door mirror, standing with her back to a toilet, titled *Mirror* (1981, fig. 5). “Overnight they went nuts, calling it despicable because her butt was next to the toilet,” Gealt remembered. “But to me the painting in the bathroom was about real life.”[6]

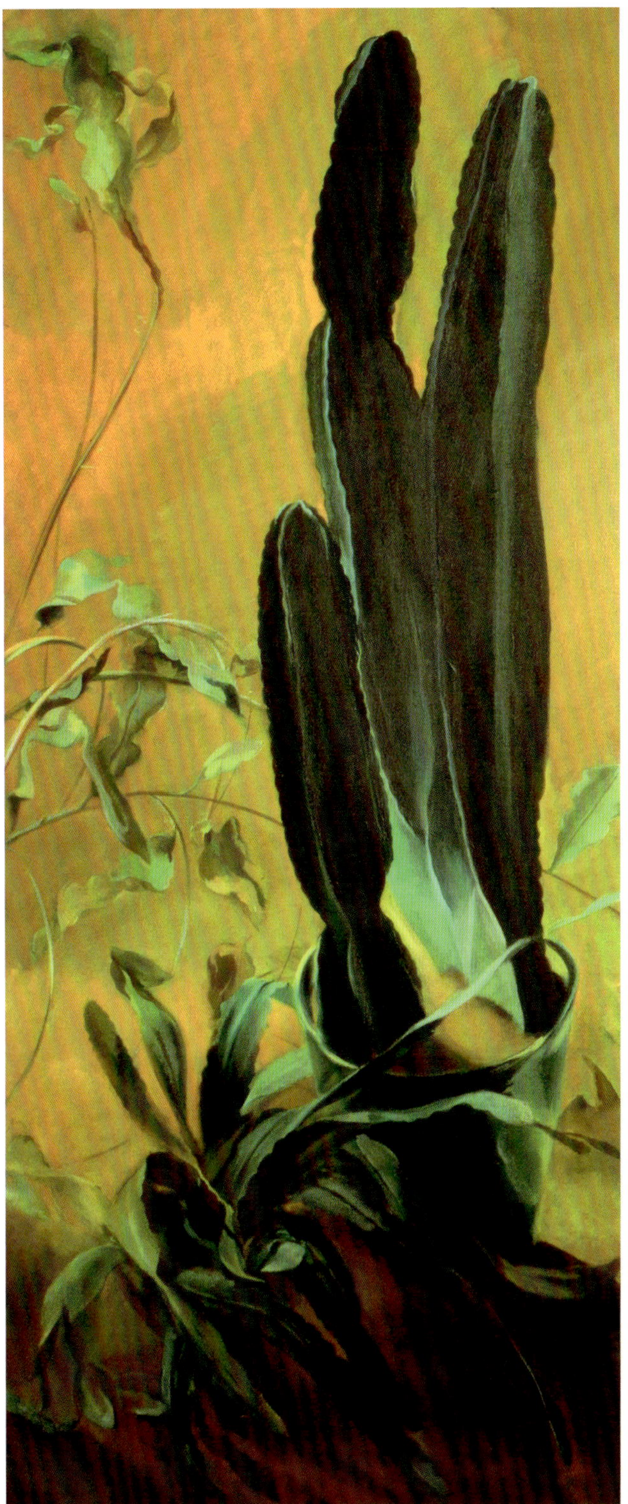

Fig. 4
Barry Gealt
Cactus, 1975
Oil on canvas
Collection of Rudolf Medicus

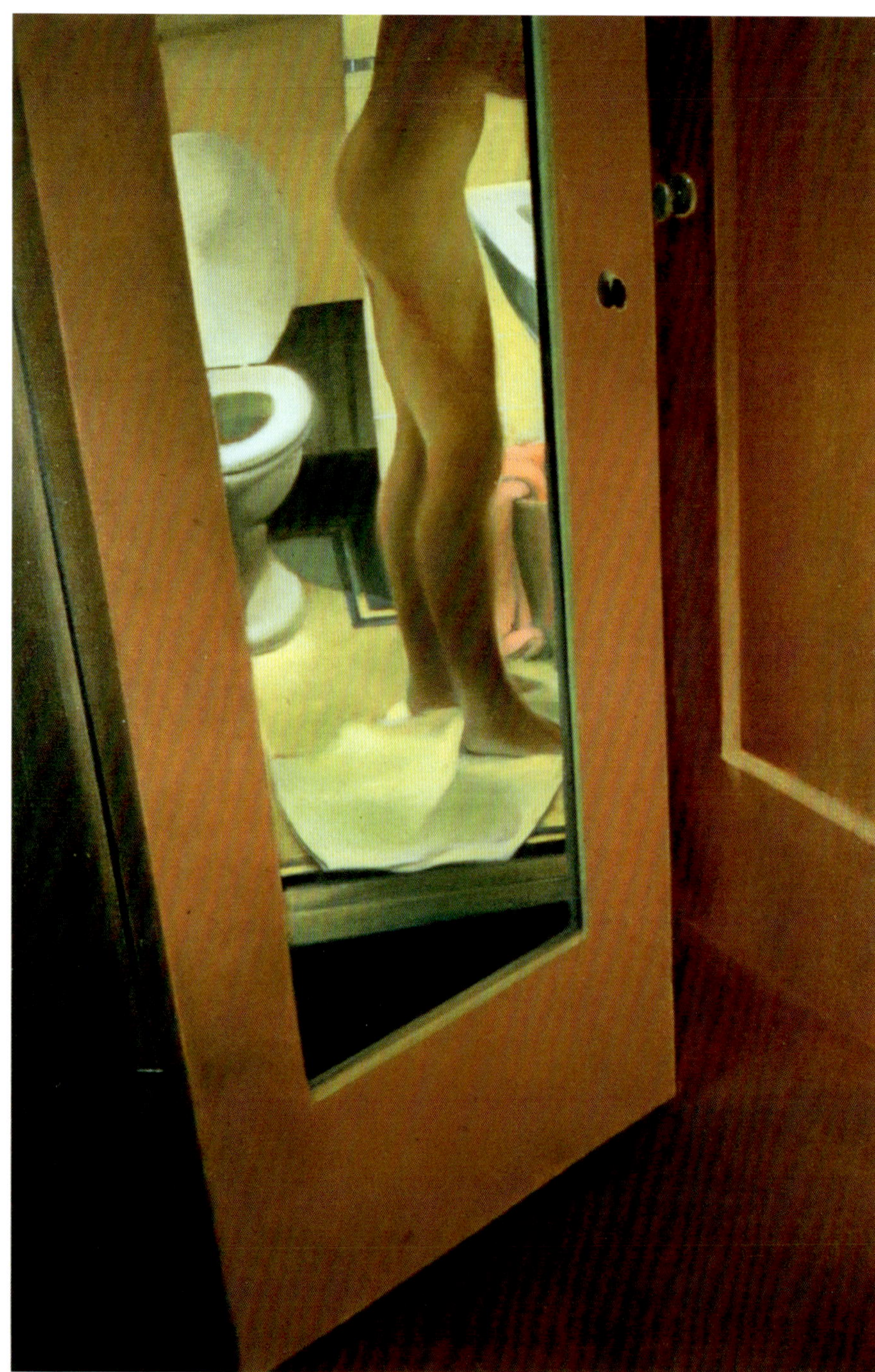

Fig. 5
Barry Gealt
Mirror, 1981
Oil on canvas
Collection of Heidi and Barry Gealt

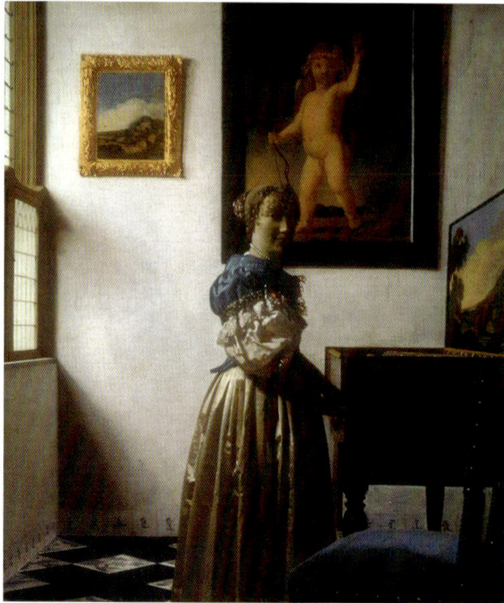

Fig. 6
Johannes Vermeer (Dutch, 1632–1675)
Lady Standing at a Virginal, ca. 1670
Oil on canvas
National Gallery, London

Fig. 7
Barry Gealt
Morning, 1984
Oil on canvas
Collection of Heidi and Barry Gealt

For Barry Gealt, the still-life and genre paintings provided a bridge between his formal training and the development of his own voice. The abstract geometry of seventeenth-century Dutch domestic interior scenes echoes in these paintings, which continued to explore the theme of contemporary people during everyday moments. Like Johannes Vermeer's *Lady Standing at a Virginal* (ca. 1670, fig. 6), the scale of the figure relative to the objects in the room created the painting's depth and space.

Gealt's painting of his wife (*Morning*, 1984, fig. 7), presents her as only an intimate partner could, rushing through her early morning routine, preparing for the day ahead. This life from the inside, from the rumpled bed sheets in the foreground, to the open closet door with its array of empty hangers, is illuminated by sunshine pouring in from an unseen window.

From the same period, *Long Train Ride* (1983, fig. 8) conjures a mood reminiscent of Edward Hopper's famous *Nighthawks* (1941). The painting's solitary figure in a physically darkened space, reflected light on metallic walls and glass, and limited palette of bold colors evoke similar feelings of loneliness in a busy, passing world. Both paintings have a universal sense of human isolation, but Gealt's complex composition, with its lack of true verticals and its creation of a truncated oblique recession at the left, places the painting solidly into a contemporary realm. *Telephone Call* (1981) is another masterful exploration of the human figure existing within a carefully circumscribed space—in this case two figures, each isolated in their separate phone booths (fig. 9).

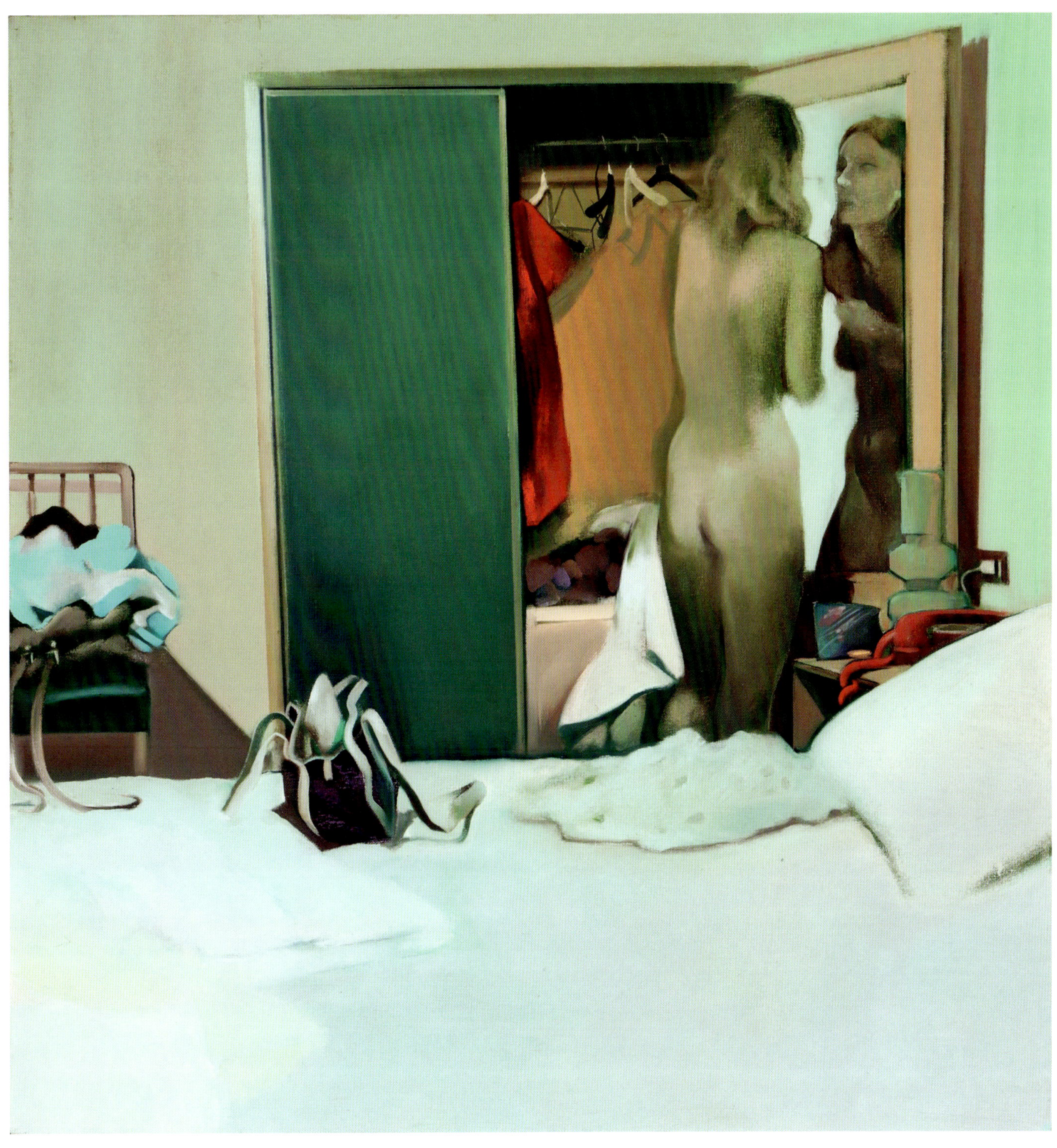

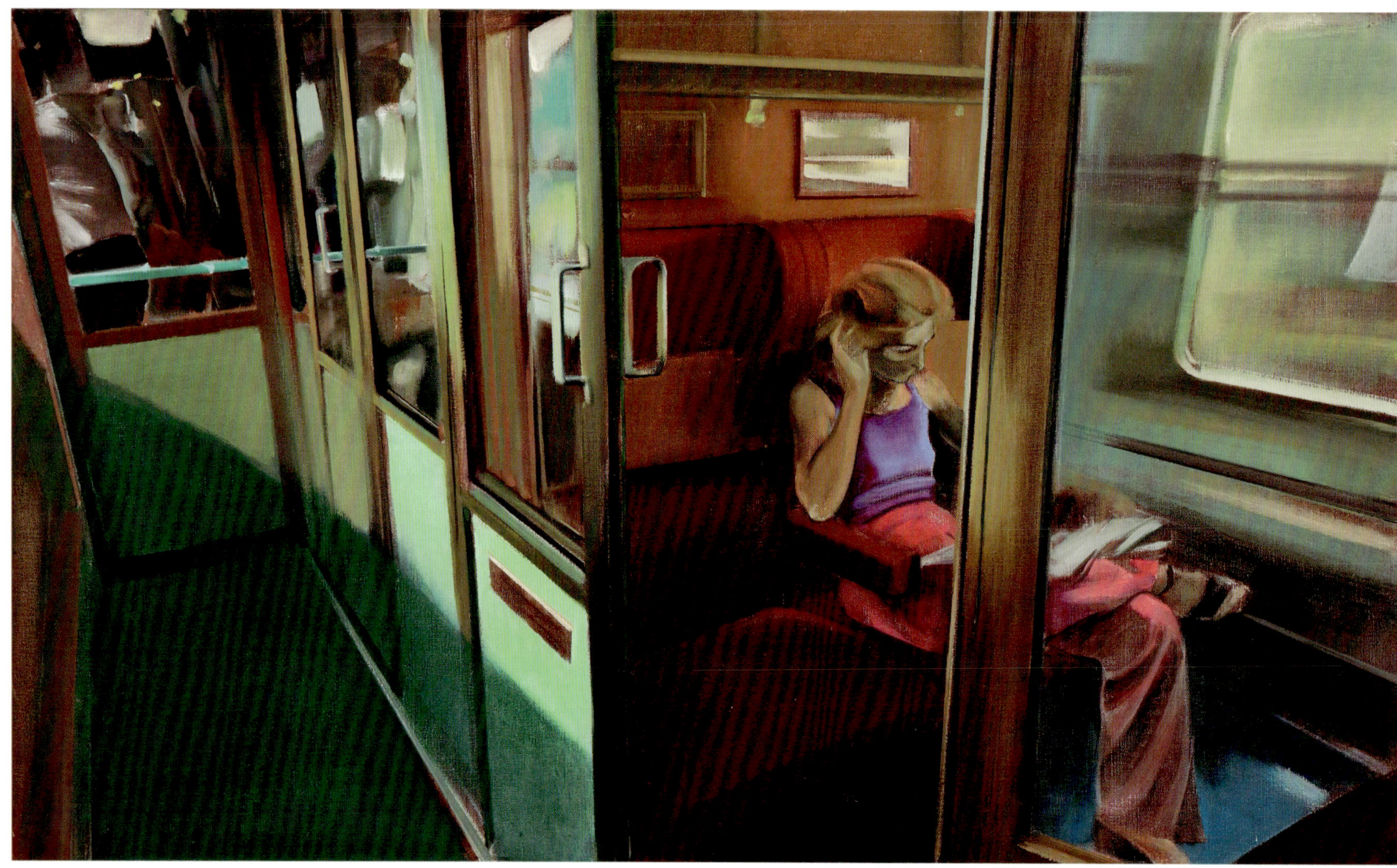

Fig. 8
Barry Gealt
Long Train Ride, 1983
Oil on canvas
Collection of Heidi and Barry Gealt

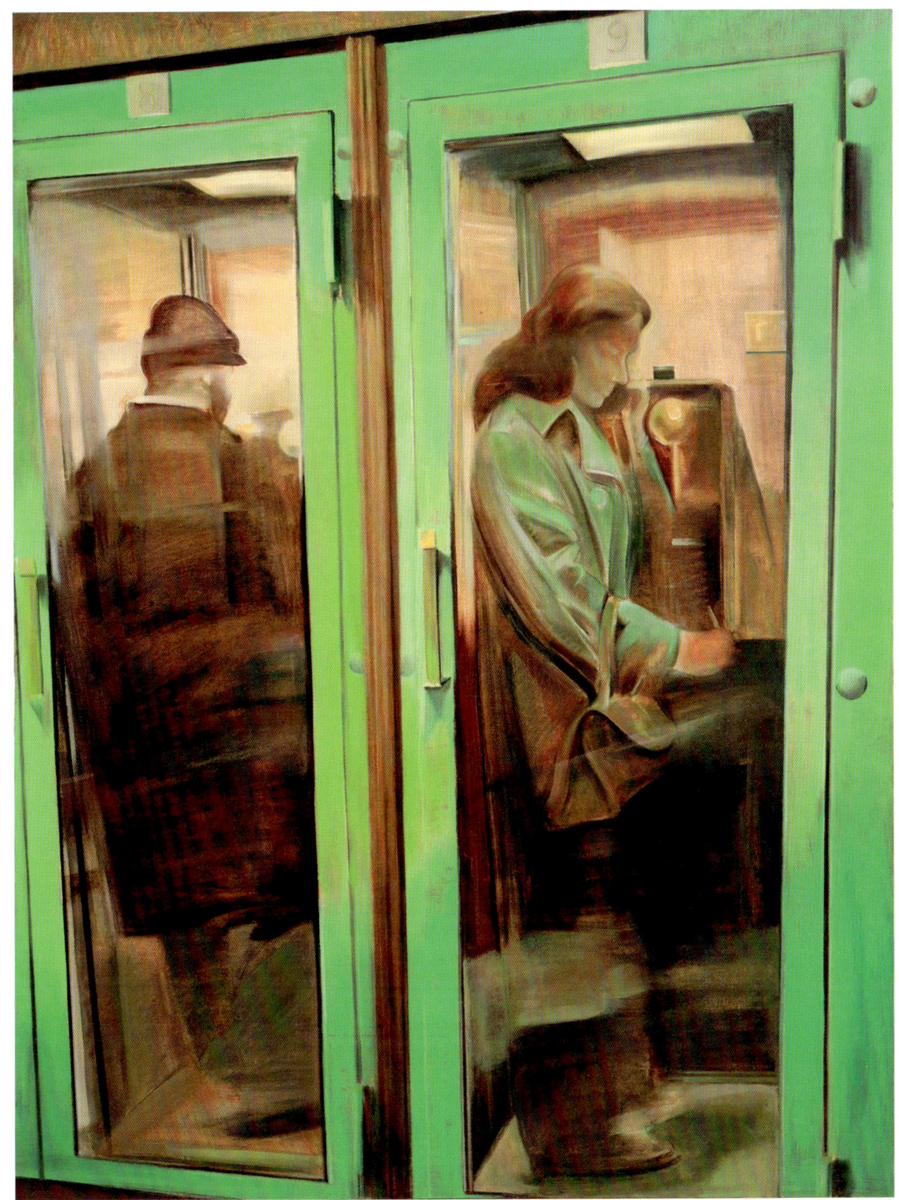

Fig. 9
Telephone Call, 1981
Oil on canvas
Collection of Robert Mann

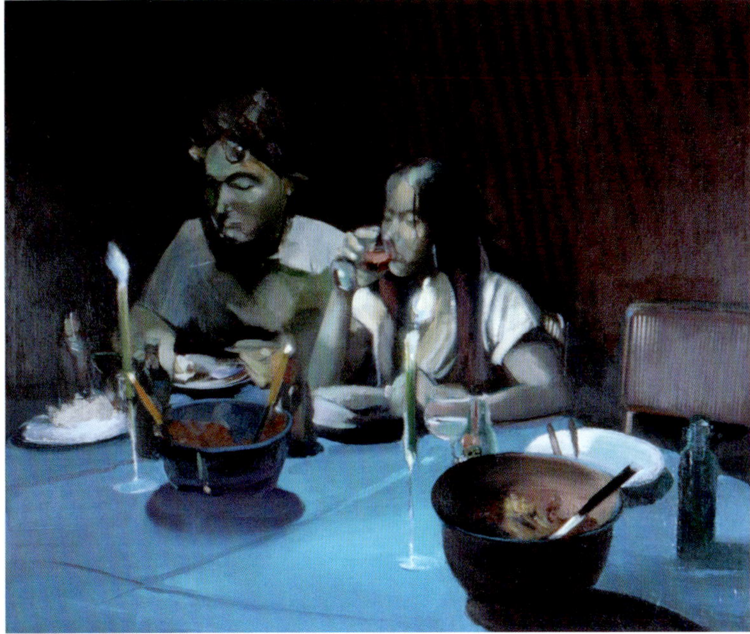

Fig. 10
Barry Gealt
Gus and Kate, 1985
Oil on canvas
Private collection

Gealt's figurative work evolved into a "dinner series" of family and friends gathered to eat, drink, and be themselves, which he composed from memory (fig. 10). He created these nighttime paintings during the day, rendering reflections of candle or lamplight on plates and glassware. Each painting is a meaningful commentary about his colleagues and relatives. The dinner paintings focused on Gealt's metaphor of home, using domestic images to convey deeply human traits—kindness, generosity, and congeniality—among a "family" of close friends and relatives.

Barry Gealt's early figurative work expressed an integral part of his personality and philosophy, with themes of humanity and kindness. When viewing Pablo Picasso's *Studio* (1934, fig. 11) in the Indiana University Art Museum, he commented on the visual symbolism while expressing empathy for the work's message:

> Here's a person fifty-four years old, painting his mistress, who's pregnant. And she's in that gigantic fleur-de-lis color—very French, purple and green, has a classical pose; and he's Spanish colors—yellow, red, blue, and he's crying. It's about age. She's twenty-one. How many people paint about age? Not a portrait of an old person, but age as an idea. Here's contrast of the young and the old. . . . I think he was one of greatest humanitarian artists we ever had.[7]

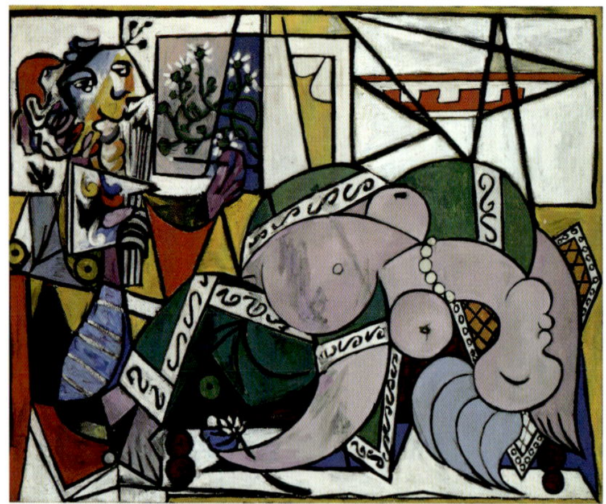

Fig. 11
Pablo Picasso (Spanish, active France, 1881–1973)
The Studio, June 1934
Oil on canvas
Gift of Dr. and Mrs. Henry R. Hope
IU Art Museum 69.55
© 2012 Estate of Pablo Picasso / Artist Rights Society (ARS), New York

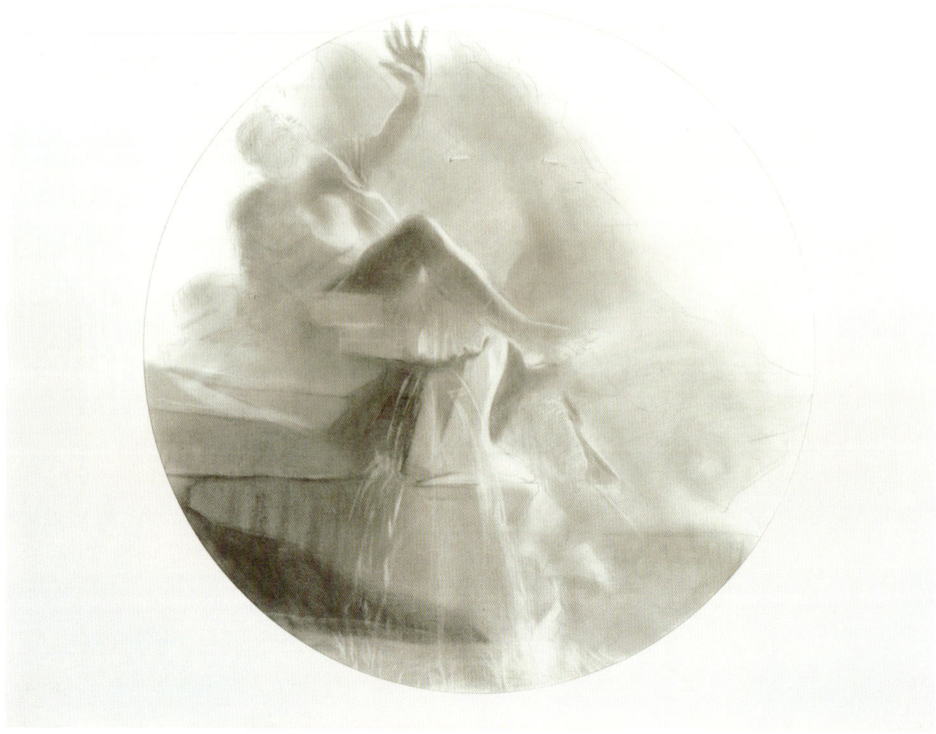

Fig. 12
Barry Gealt
Bernini Fountain, Rome, 1979
Graphite on paper
Collection of Heidi and Barry Gealt

But to Gealt, the family and dinner paintings reflected the subjects, and not the painter. "I wanted [to convey] humanity and kindness, but I was still an artist painting someone else."[8] While continuing to teach during the 1980s, he took a two-year hiatus from his figurative work.

Accompanying his wife to Florence, Italy, for her summer research, Gealt ventured out each day, making pencil drawings of statues, fountains, and small urban landscapes. These sensitive drawings, and later, multi-layered studio prints, freed him to explore visual ideas without making the commitment of paint on canvas (fig. 12). "I didn't want to paint people anymore," he explained,

> I wanted to paint who I was… The artists I liked [such as Courbet] were about the artist painting the painting, not the people in the painting. Landscapes seemed to be the vehicle to be an artist. Figure paintings generate stories [about the figures]. In landscapes, words become less important.[9]

To be an artist of his own time continued to be one of Gealt's essential aspirations:

> I don't want to be anybody but myself and I want to be a contemporary artist. You have to fight to be one, because art really does change every decade. And it's not that you can make changes to be contemporary. You have to be part of life in a contemporary way. And that's important to me. I don't want to paint things that look like another era. I want to look like I belong right now.[10]

One of Gealt's artistic heroes, Gustav Courbet, who led the Realist movement in nineteenth-century French painting, believed it could not be otherwise: "The artists of one century [are] basically incapable of reproducing the aspect of a past or future century." For Courbet, the only possible source for a living art was the artist's own experience.[11]

Barry Gealt as Teacher

One way Barry Gealt keeps his own art vital and alive is through his interaction with his young students (fig. 13). Being a teacher of painting is an integral part of who Barry Gealt is. His years of giving of himself and his knowledge have shaped and solidified his own opinions in addition to influencing innumerable emerging artists.

> I find it extremely important and almost an obligation to help young artists who make every endeavor to stay in our field. That is the way I was treated by artists in school and in professional life, and I want to pass that generosity of spirit on to young artists. I hope in turn that they will also help other artists whenever possible.[12]

Gealt's efforts to broaden horizons for his students included organizing and raising funds for students' travel abroad. Beginning a program for fine art undergraduates in 1981, initially part of Indiana University's Overseas Study program, he was able to help a total of 320 undergraduates and 160 graduate students to participate in his classes, which took place in Italy or France during summers over the next twenty-five years (fig. 14).

A former graduate student of Barry Gealt's, Matthew Ballou, who now teaches at the University of Missouri, wholeheartedly adopted his mentor's philosophy of giving. "This is something that has since become a huge part of how I teach," he wrote in August 2011.

> Barry thought of this generosity of spirit in two primary ways. First, he saw it as consciously extending goodwill toward other artists. This meant acknowledging that when an artist is in the studio, working hard, spending time with ideas and words and actions and images, they deserve some true consideration and an assumption that they're not just working to deceive a gullible audience. People who really dedicate years of their life to art-making aren't doing it just to craft a lame inside joke; they're doing it because they love it, believe in it, and have made huge sacrifices to make it a part of their lives. Barry claimed that sacrifice deserves both respect and the generosity of believing the best about someone making it. It was because of the tremendous value he saw in the art-making life that Barry was willing to be forceful and confrontational with his grads; he wanted us to be worthy of the respect he had for the work and us.

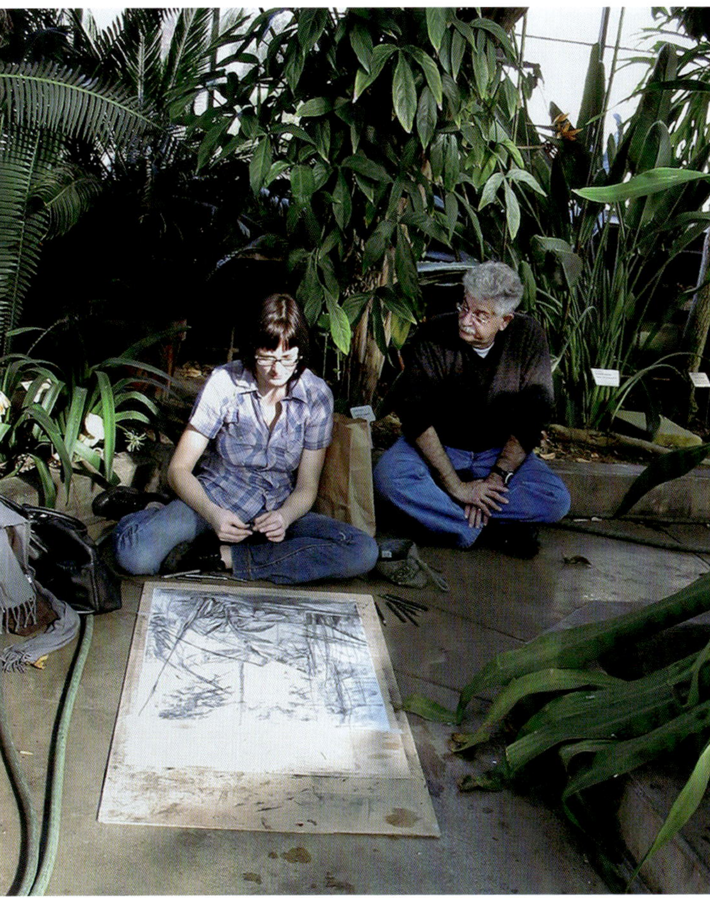

Fig. 13
Barry Gealt and Dani Orchard at the IU Greenhouse, 2007

> Secondly, Barry expressed his notion of generosity of spirit as a kind of networking principle. Not as a crass, dog-eat-dog use of people just to get ahead of the competition, nor as *quid pro quo*. To Barry, generosity of spirit meant taking initiative to actively create opportunities for others and, in so doing, create a culture of opportunity for oneself. This went beyond doing something nice just to get something nice in return. It was a lifestyle choice meant to create a reciprocal community of support and encouragement. With enough people involved, each giving and receiving in a way beyond 'you scratch my back, I'll scratch yours,' a sea change in the human equation would take place and grace would abound.[13]

Despite his generosity toward other artists, Gealt has never minced words during critiques nor softened his opinion toward students who aren't serious about making art. Ballou wrote, "He detested lackadaisical studio practice. He roared against artworks that evinced an artist's lack of desire to press deep into the process and lifestyle of serious creative effort. He reacted strongly against anything he interpreted as denying or limiting the sort of committed engagement that motivated his own work and teaching."[14]

Students who responded to Gealt's teaching methods are reverent with their praise. Ballou stated, "My relationship with Barry Gealt was the most important and influential of those I had with colleagues and professors while at Indiana University for grad school.... He trained me to take this lifestyle seriously, to be committed to it in a dynamic, spiritual way. In this he made me a better, more thoughtful person and a more knowing citizen of the world.... In spite of all his bluster Barry loved us and showed us grace and encouragement."[15]

Former graduate student Christine Mugnulo said of Gealt's teaching, "He infused the [studio] process with an exhilarating, liberating sense of living. He taught us the difference between making and creating."[16] Another student mentored by Gealt, Karrie Maxwell, remembered, "Studio visits with Barry left me invigorated, with a sense of pride and initiative to be daring, courageous; to be innovative and different. This is what was and is so special about Barry. He encourages you to be yourself—Boldly."[17] Rachel Welling, a participant in several trips abroad with Gealt wrote, "Barry was a saving grace as a teacher because he always prized the student's concepts. In critiques, his commentary was often bombastic, unpredictable, provocative, and humorous. We could count on him to raise the level of expectation and achievement."[18]

Gealt keeps track of his former students' and colleagues' thoughts and ideas through ongoing e-mail and phone conversations with them. He commented, "What is most intriguing is seeing the birth of new ideas and new images and new ways in the presenting and the making of art. Change is inevitable. It is always challenging and exciting, if not at times downright frightening. But change can only vitalize our ideas and what our work means."[19] Changes in an artist's work do not come about solely from years of experimentation with their chosen mediums, but they are also a function of personal development. Human beings don't remain the same throughout their lives. Layers of experiences crystallize our opinions and shape us into who we are at this moment. An artist's favorite work is often his most recent, since it embodies the culmination of his skills and expresses who he currently is.

During Gealt's self-imposed hiatus from oil painting in the early 1980s, he found himself drawn to the philosophy and aesthetics of Japanese artwork, including the comprehensive Buddhist world view known as *wabi-sabi*, which "nurtures all that is authentic by acknowledging three simple realities: nothing lasts, nothing is finished, and nothing is perfect."[20] Later, Gealt was able to explore Japanese sensibilities first-hand when granted a Lilly Endowment Fellowship to Japan in the early 1990s. Although, in the Japanese language, *wabi* and *sabi* both contain undertones of desolation and solitude, Gealt interprets the concept to mean imperfect, accidental beauty—unpretentious, simple, and intimate. To create something significantly beautiful out of complete nothingness is the ultimate expression of this concept for him:

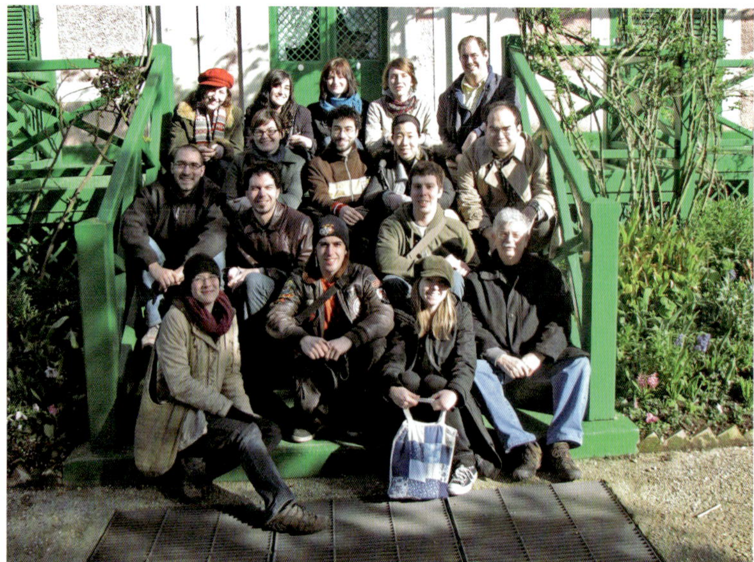

Fig. 14
Barry Gealt with IU B.F.A. students in Giverny, France, spring break 2007

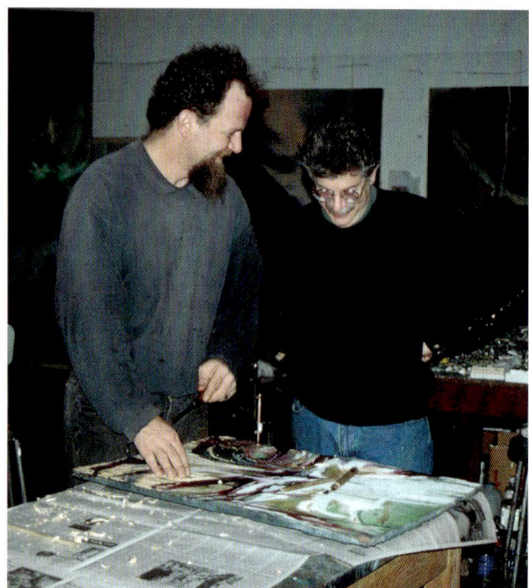

Fig. 15
Barry Gealt and former MFA student Nick Hill work on a woodcut in the Spencer studio, 1992

"To paint nothing makes you paint something. It's up to the artist to bring your burdens to your work. The things that could be nothing become meaningful. Conversely, to paint something [in close detail], you turn it into nothing. Style should never be first."[21] As an example, he cites the unassuming waterfall in his backyard that becomes a frothing cascade in a zigzag ravine of shiny wet earth and boulders in his waterfall paintings.

Pursuing his delight in natural phenomena, Gealt applied for and received grants and fellowships abroad, which allowed him to "paint where heroes painted." He won a Terra Foundation 2003 summer residency in Giverny, France, and a 2005 Indiana University College of Arts and Humanities Institute Research Grant to Normandy. Artists such as Claude Monet (1840–1926), Gustave Courbet (1819–1877), and J. M. W. Turner (1775–1851), inform his views of how artists meet their own challenges.

Embracing the Landscape

In 1973 the Gealts moved to an old farmstead in rural Owen County, about twenty miles from Bloomington, and, over time, in his life in the country he found the authentic artistic vision he had sought.

> I can't really pin down what happened with the big change-over to landscape—the move to Owen Valley [rural Owen County] and experiencing the foggy mornings, hiking in the woods, mushroom hunting, and cutting down trees.... Your whole concept [while] living in the city—people were important. But when you live in the country, nature becomes important. I never thought of painting landscape before. But it allowed me to paint in a way I wanted to paint.[22]

Confronting his heroes on his own terms, Gealt's initial landscapes developed from his Indiana experience. Where Monet preferred to paint controlled nature, Gealt looked to the shaggy hills of Sweet Owen Valley. Like Turner, he wanted to capture the reality of a place that transcends mere depiction. These paintings of his homestead reflect the windless mists of Indiana mornings and the hush and rustle of winter woods.

By the late 1980s, he had turned his attention to the waterfall on his property, rendering it in large, bold, semi-abstract canvases. Late fall walks, where the burbling waterfall brought vibrancy to the already subdued autumn landscape, evolved into *November* (1991, fig. 16), reinforcing Gealt's growing sensitivity to his home place.

His trip to Japan in 1992/93 inspired his work the following winter. Gealt grew tired of "painting logic." He wanted to paint disparate elements, where "color has weight and does not rely on drawing; where small amounts of some colors are larger than big amounts of other colors; where the activity of painting is as important as the image."[23] He applied himself to making prints as a collaborative medium to hone his technical creative process (fig. 15).

His prints are like no others. Spreading layer upon layer of color, he created thick, earthy, almost sculptural slabs. Often making horizontal or vertical diptychs, as with *Ancient Memories Unleashed* (1992, fig. 17), he transformed two-dimensional sheets of paper into stunningly luscious, tactile objects.

His fearless approach to the woodcuts informed the radically impasto style of his oils on canvas, and majestic, foreboding places emerged. *The Cave* (1994, fig. 18, see also p. 28) dives into a bottomless fissure where acidic green and yellow reflect off the receding rock sides. We're already sliding into the abyss with no chance at grabbing a root or tree branch. Perhaps symbolic of Plato's Cave, we see the irregular limestone wall only as brilliant color—an artist's sublime vision of life on earth. A breakthrough in boldness, the *Reddening Glow of Night* (1994, fig. 19, see also p. 29), inspired by the red clay soil, brings high drama to volcanic light disappearing behind a molten hill.

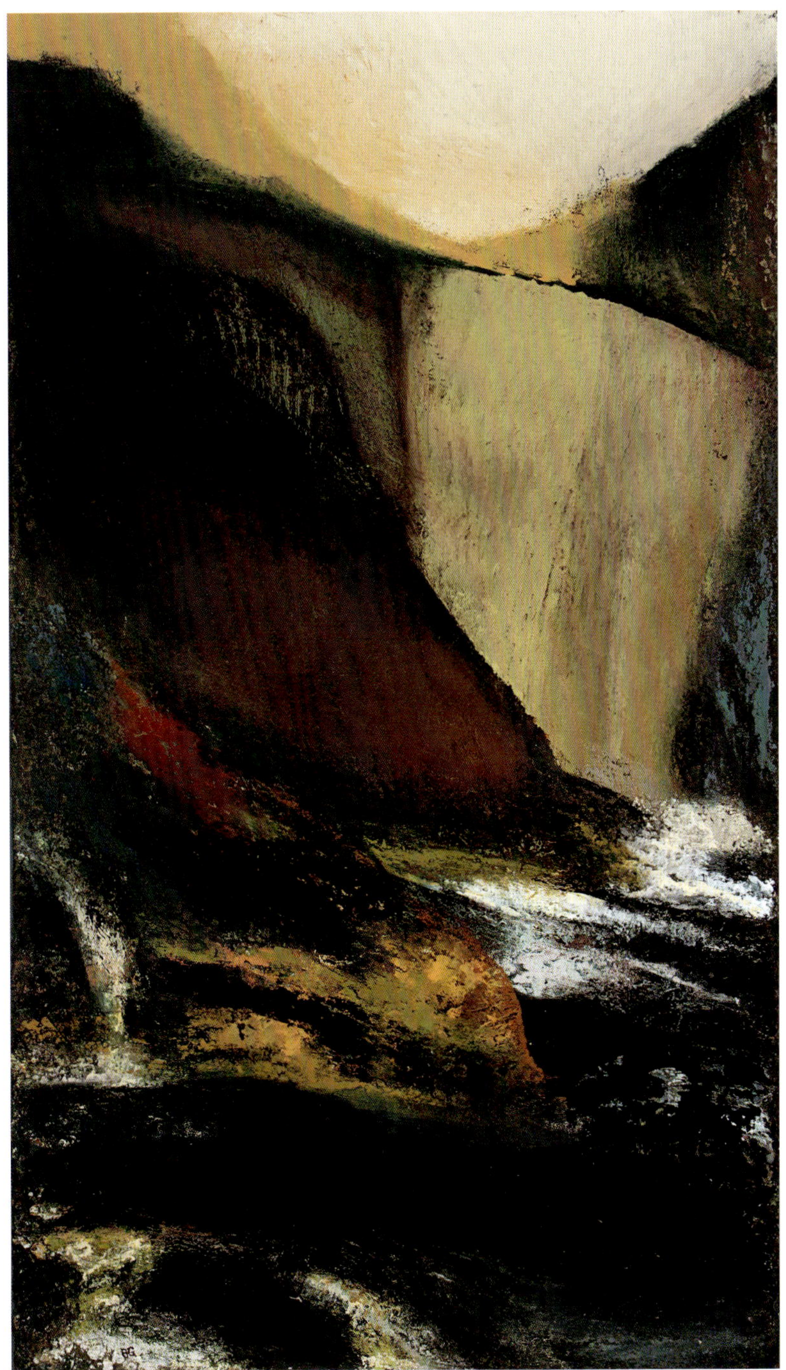

Fig. 16
Barry Gealt
November, 1991
Oil on canvas
Collection of Anthony J. Moravec
Columbus, Indiana

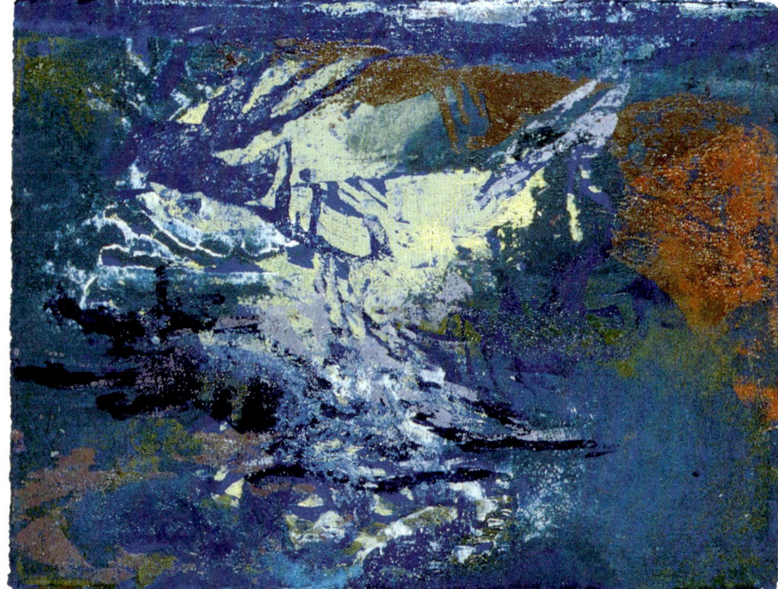

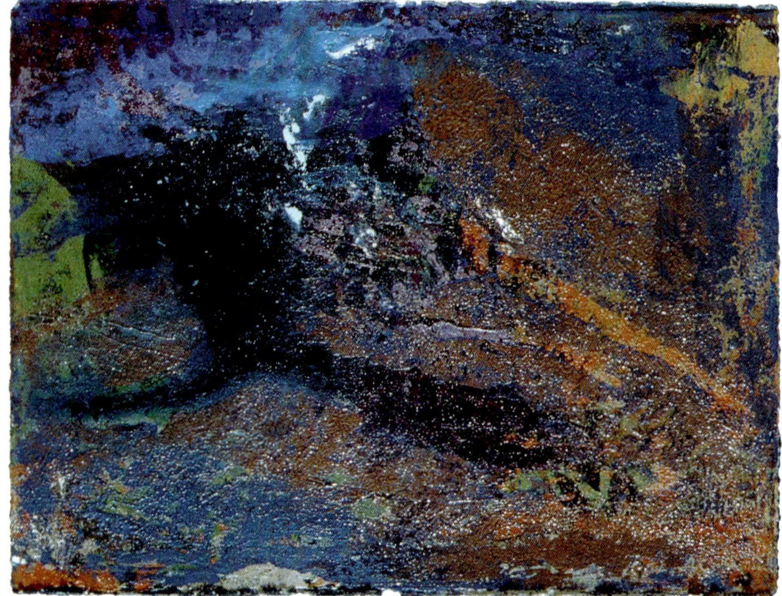

Fig. 17
Barry Gealt
Ancient Memories Unleashed, 1992
Woodcut diptych
Private collection

Barry Gealt takes small simple things and makes them important by ignoring horizons and detailed descriptions of confined scenes.

> Making art over a long period of time, you learn more and more about what you're doing. There's nothing really magnificent about what I'm painting, but if you paint the essence of the place, it does become magnificent. Painting, whether it's Indiana or wherever I choose to paint, I'm inspired by seeing the things that I see.... These are bombastic paintings but of little places.[24]

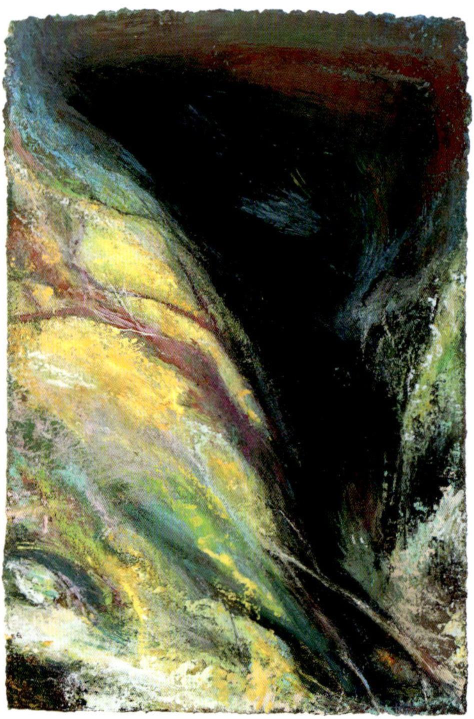

Fig. 18
Barry Gealt
The Cave, 1994
Oil on canvas
Collection of Anthony J. Moravec
Columbus, Indiana

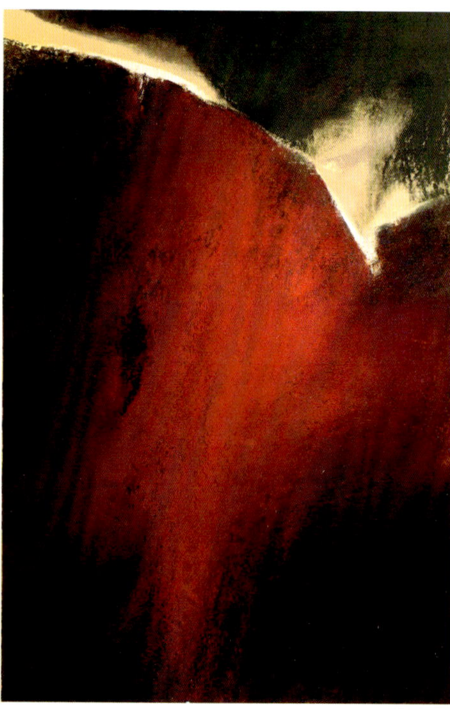

Fig. 19
Barry Gealt
The Reddening Glow of Night, 1994
Oil on canvas
Collection of Thies Knauf, Shelbyville

Southern Indiana in winter, with its cloud-muffled days and naked tree skeletons marching up hills of drab brown and ochre, is a time of hibernation and contemplation, as in *Indiana Vista* (p. 48) and *Forest Edge III* (both 2001, fig. 20). Early spring insinuates itself by gradually replacing freezing rain with thawing ground and hints of newly minted green. Colors made bolder by their surrounding hues bring intensity to the splashing turbulence of *Muddy Hill* (2001, fig. 21).

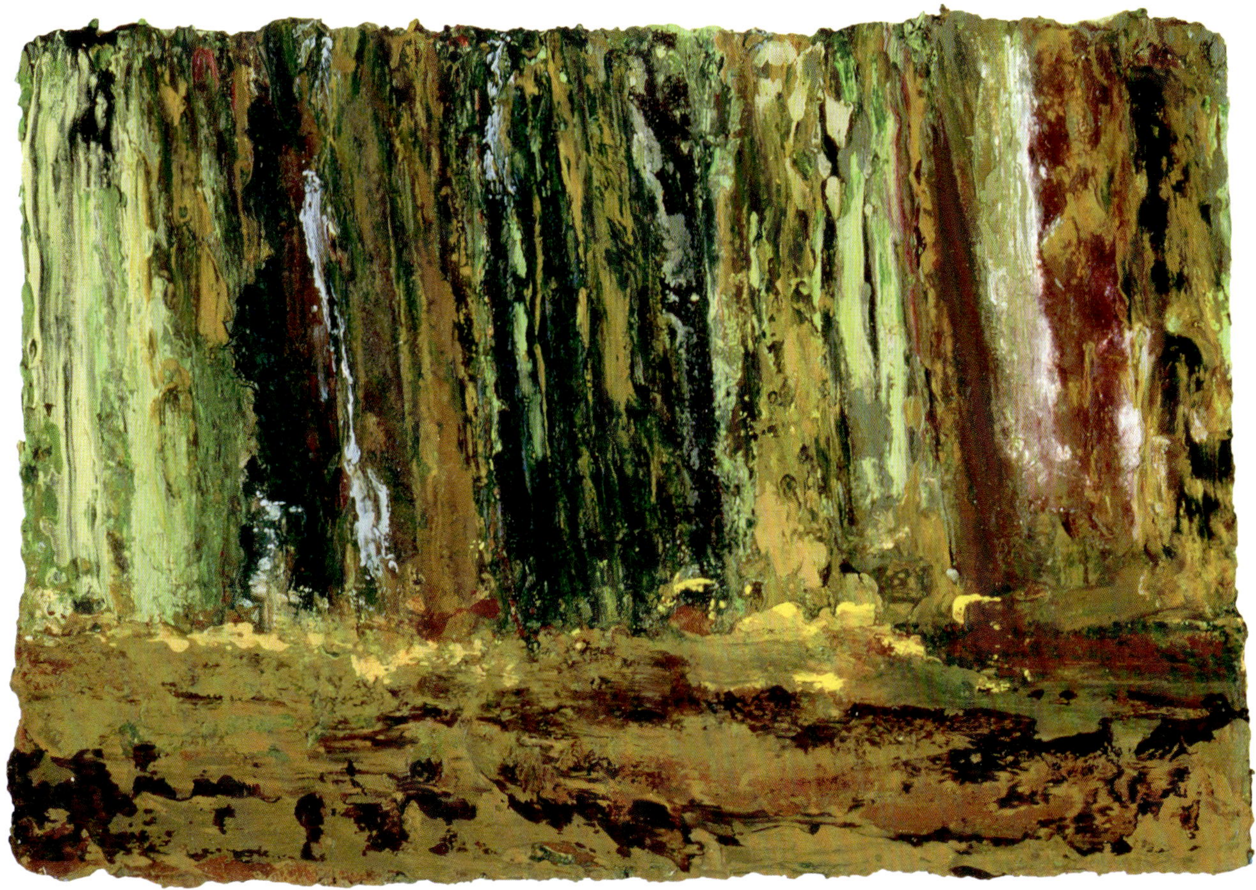

Fig. 20
Barry Gealt
Forest Edge III, 2001
Oil on canvas
Courtesy Osper Gallery, Cologne, Germany

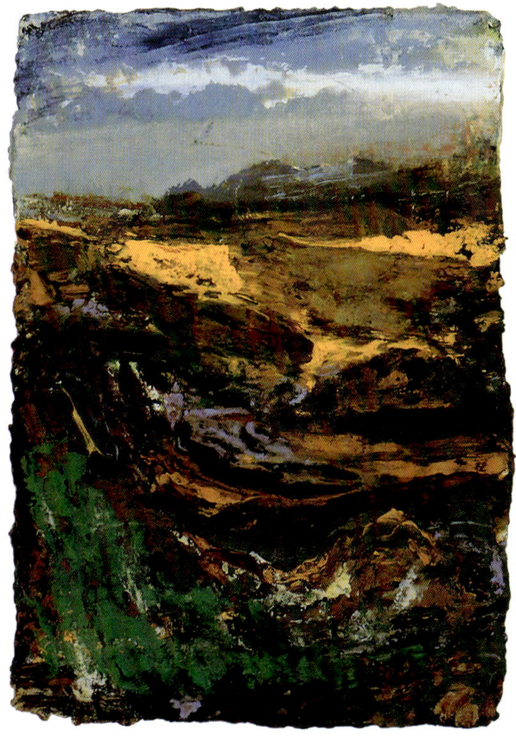

Fig. 21
Barry Gealt
Muddy Hill, 2001
Oil on canvas
Collection of Marion Knauf, Berlin, Germany

Paint, in Gealt's hands, becomes an almost sculptural medium. He immerses himself in the building up of the painting surface—pouring, scooping, using his hands or palette knife, or whatever instrument serves his purpose. Where tools were previously insignificant to his artwork, they become all-important. The rough, spontaneous paint surface is the first thing that attracts and engulfs viewers. "Paint has to be an issue for me," he says. "Paint isn't something just to make a pretty shape. It isn't to become a rendered form.... Out of the paint, miraculously, something appears...."[25]

His sculptured surface is often built with deliciously radical color: patches of salmon highlighting wet rocks in *Waterfall II* (2001, fig. 22); bubble-gum pink and lemon yellow accenting the sun streaked currents in *Approaching the Falls* (2003, fig. 23); diagonal swaths of deep rose-maroon against hot green and black in *Paradise Valley, Utah* (fig. 24, see also p. 39) from a trip out west in 2005. His emphasis on surface, material, and color has not only developed along with his progression of ideas, but it arises out of the intrinsic possibilities of his medium—thick, juicy paint.

The pieces exude Gealt's energy and joy. They look like he had fun creating them. He comments about the process, "All those textures; the way the colors mix—I try to make magic. If I walk into the studio and the painting is dull, [it must be reworked]. I've already put so much time into it, so what's another week or month?"[26]

In the summer of 2003, Gealt first visited Etretat, on the northern coast of Normandy. "I couldn't believe I was actually there," he wrote. "[It's] a place of ancient conflicts, artistic mentors, and wartime heroes. Artists have been drawn there to create incredible images for many decades. I never could have expected the effect it would have on me. How do you create works of art from a place so well known? How do you pay homage to your heroes?"[27]

For four years he painted from his memory "of the changing temperature of light and weather and differing heights of the cliffs and being in the belly of the swell of the waves," culminating in a 2007 show of five paintings at a Montreal gallery. Soaring above the famous cliffs and looking down as a seagull might, soft greens and browns of flat terrain in *Etretat I* (fig. 25, see also p. 43) lead to abrupt vertical cream-colored rock cliffs sweeping down to the lavender-gray sea, and *Etretat II* (see p. 42) again from aloft, taking in muscular dark jade and cobalt waves swelling into white caps, with a hint of horizon in the upper left corner. Gealt's Étretat euphoria is palpable.

He returned in spirit to his more serene Midwestern home in 2007, revisiting views seen by earth-bound humans; watching earth's revolving daily dance from bright to dim. The horizon became important. He commented, "I've always had the notion that at the horizon, you don't know what lies ahead. I love that idea—that we don't know what lies ahead. It's a metaphor for painting. It's always been a struggle, and you don't know where you're struggling to get to.... You don't know where it's taking you."[28]

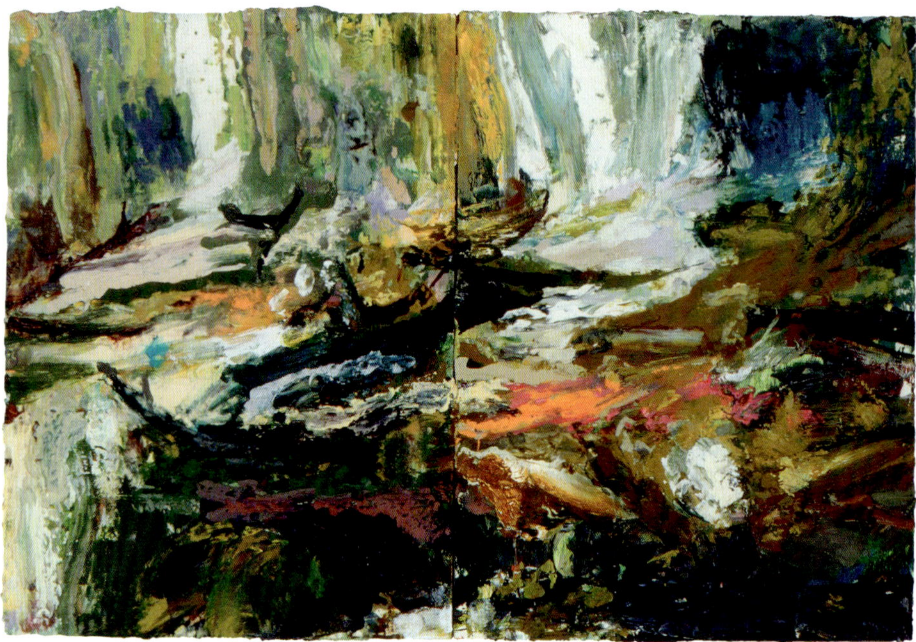

Fig. 22
Barry Gealt
Waterfall II, 2001
Oil on panel
Courtesy Kunsthandlung Osper,
Cologne, Germany

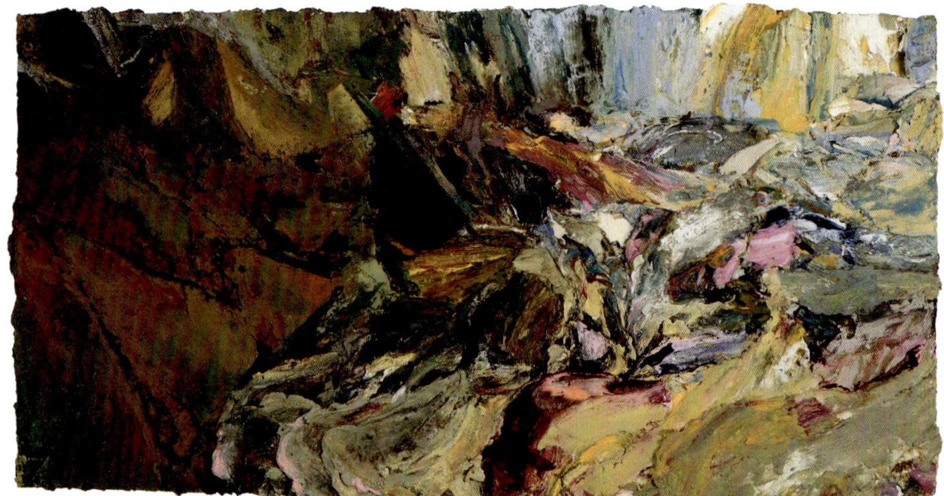

Fig. 23
Barry Gealt
Approaching the Falls, 2003
Oil on panel
Collection of Wally Goodman and Patrick Duffy

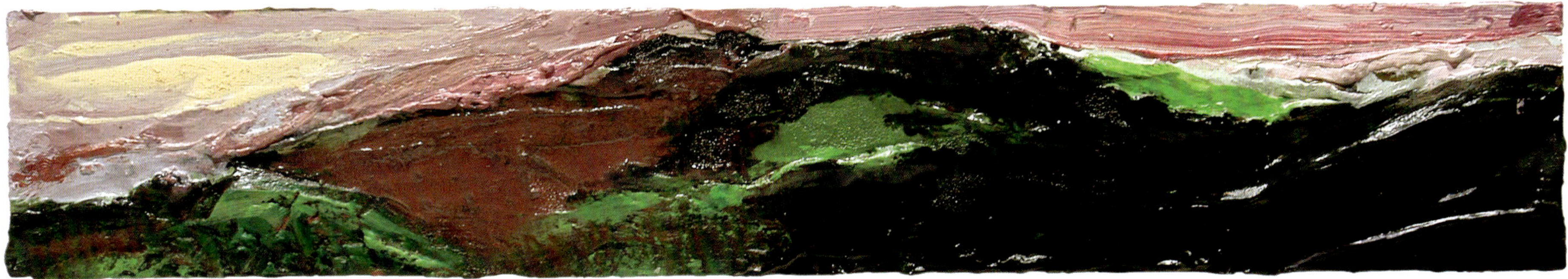

Fig. 24
Barry Gealt
Paradise Valley, Utah, 2005
Oil on panel
Private collection of Gabriele and Dieter Bamberger, Cologne, Germany

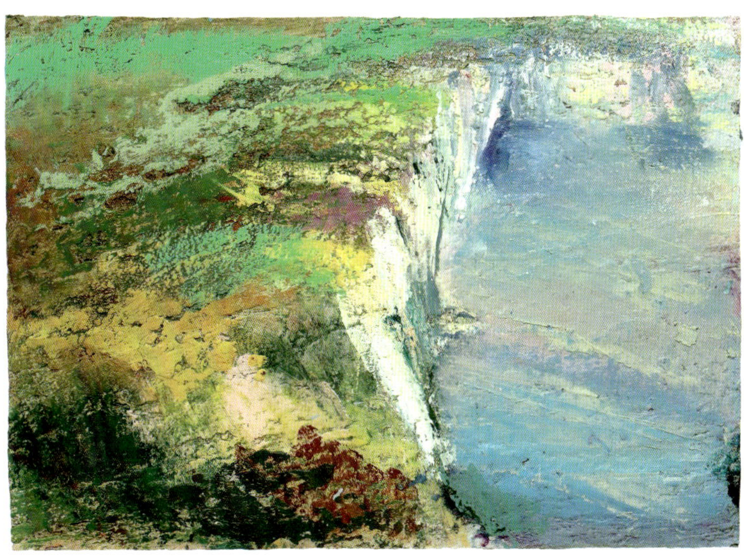

Fig. 25
Barry Gealt
Etretat I, 2007
Oil on canvas mounted on board
Collection of Ann and Rusty Harrison

Building the Paintings

The significance of the horizon developed into extremely horizontal formats. One of a series of three canvases (each 13 ½" x 85 ½"), *Early Evening Sunset I* (2007, see pp. 44–45) throbs with peach and warm yellow radiance behind a bumpy, dark maroon hill. Scrape, form, deposit; layer after layer—the essence of the place stripped naked from a potentially pictorial painting. There are no attempts at 3-D trickery using color temperature, values, or scale to create visual depth.

The physical building of the paintings is no small task. Forget purchasing paint in mere tubes. Gealt orders his oil paint in cans. Sometimes panels weighing more than one hundred pounds necessitate working on flat tables. Painting flat on tables is conducive to more abstract concepts, eliminating the tendency fostered by conventional upright easels to visually frame a painting. Like some Abstract Expressionists, who dropped their paints onto floor-canvases, Gealt is looking down at his work, tipping the ground to pour paint down the top of a waterfall, or scraping mounds of wet oil paint to one side to reveal an underlayer. Periodically, the painting must be manhandled upright to view as a wall piece.

The physical struggle in the studio is evident even in the calmest of Gealt's Indiana landscapes, which seems to conflate the turbulence of modern times with the ever-intensifying forces of nature. Perhaps in response to the twenty-first-century tsunami or earthquakes, a vaguely apprehensive feeling underlies the silence of heavy skies and veils of morning fog in *Early November Fog, Owen Valley* (2008, fig. 26). *Distant Waterfall* (fig. 28, see also p. 33), a composition divided by a vertical brown tree trunk slicing the distant waterfall from the earth-toned shapes and worn rocks, gives the viewer two viewpoints, a metaphor for our close little world affected by global events. "When you look at one of my paintings, I want you to see a perfect world," Gealt said. "But inside that world you may also see upheaval, solitude, a sense of daring and of the unknown. There are no footholds, no people. It's just nature and my thoughts pushed out into nature. Making a perfect world doesn't mean it's all happy."[29]

In his second series presenting the sea, inspired by a trip to Canada's Prince Edward Island in 2009, the horizon continued to be all-important (fig. 27). Gealt's massively wide paintings evoke the drama of the place: rushing thump of dark purple waves splashing over shell-pink sands; hot rose streaks describing the

Fig. 26
Barry Gealt
Early November Fog, Owen County, 2008
Oil on panel
From the collection of the Indiana State Museum and Historic Sites

undertow of shallow water; shapes of volcanic ship-wrecking rocks; sea-scented tide pools and racing storm clouds. In startlingly realistic evocations of what it feels like to be there, we experience the tang of seaweed, gusts of wind, and sea foam flecking our cheeks. Gealt declares, "I have an idea of place when I begin. A painting can't be a piece of something. You're painting a place, not a piece of a place. It's important to make the painting so you're at that place."[30]

To Gealt, landscape painting removes all words to create a true visual experience. But, unlike those who go out into nature to capture this essence, he explores his impressions of places back in the studio. "Making art and making pictures are two different things," he declares. "When you're doing a plein air [on location] painting, you're using all your skills, but you can't think that the horizon line is time. For [plein-air painters], they are capturing the moment, and can't be invested in something incredible."[31]

How to capture the essence of nature? Perhaps John Wells (1907–2000), one of the St. Ives circle of British modernists, said it best: "But how can one paint the warmth of the sun, the sound of the sea, the journey of a beetle across a rock, or thoughts of one's own whence and whither? That's one argument for abstraction. One absorbs all these feelings and ideas; if one is lucky they undergo an alchemistic transformation into gold and that is creative work."[32]

Gealt's process involves several paintings as he absorbs and interprets places, at home and while traveling, sometimes starting as many as eight panels in the studio at once. "The studio allows me to use my ability to maneuver and wrestle with the materials and ideas."[33] His ideas grow out of other paintings. Each painting feeds the next, encouraging exploration and new discoveries. Gealt is not interested in the surface impressions of a scene, but what's underneath. What's the visceral feeling when physically there? What forces predominate, causing gut response and conveying life's struggle?

Traveling to Maine in 2010 sustained his passion for the rough and craggy coast of the Eastern seaboard. Like one of his earliest heroes, Winslow Homer, Gealt paints monumental seascapes; crashing waves and salty foam; distant light reflected from the ocean surface. But Homer treated paintings in a pictorial way, making the viewer a safe observer. Gealt takes us to the water's edge, where we know potential danger. "You can't swim in my oceans," he admits.

The paintings have grown even larger (several are over eight feet long). Their cold blue and turquoise water, sky streaked with contrasting pale gemlike color, putty grays and volcanic black rocks, command any gallery. The recent landscapes are specifically titled, as in *Low Tide, Outer Bar Island, 8:30 am*, *Corea, Maine* (2010, fig. 29, see also pp. 62–63). He explained,

> I am naming the specific places now—I want these locations to get the credit they deserve.... It is exciting to see a day unfold from the morning to evening. The reflections of light on rocks and water to the enormous sunrises and evening sunsets: all this seems to move at a speed that reflects the rushing of ongoing time. The landscape constantly transforms itself through the day to reflect emotions from joyousness to melancholy, and stages from growth to decay. Each day embraces nature's predictable yet unique events. I want to share in these experiences....[34]

Despite their apparent specificity, the paintings are elevated beyond the particular to the universal forces of nature, time, and the eventual end of all things as we know them.

Gealt's shared experiences resonate with many. His forceful landscapes dominate rooms in locales such as New Mexico, Florida, Maine, Montreal, Cologne and Germany, and, of course, Indiana. Some collectors treasure his pensive canvases, while others choose the more spectacular works. In one such painting, *Raging*

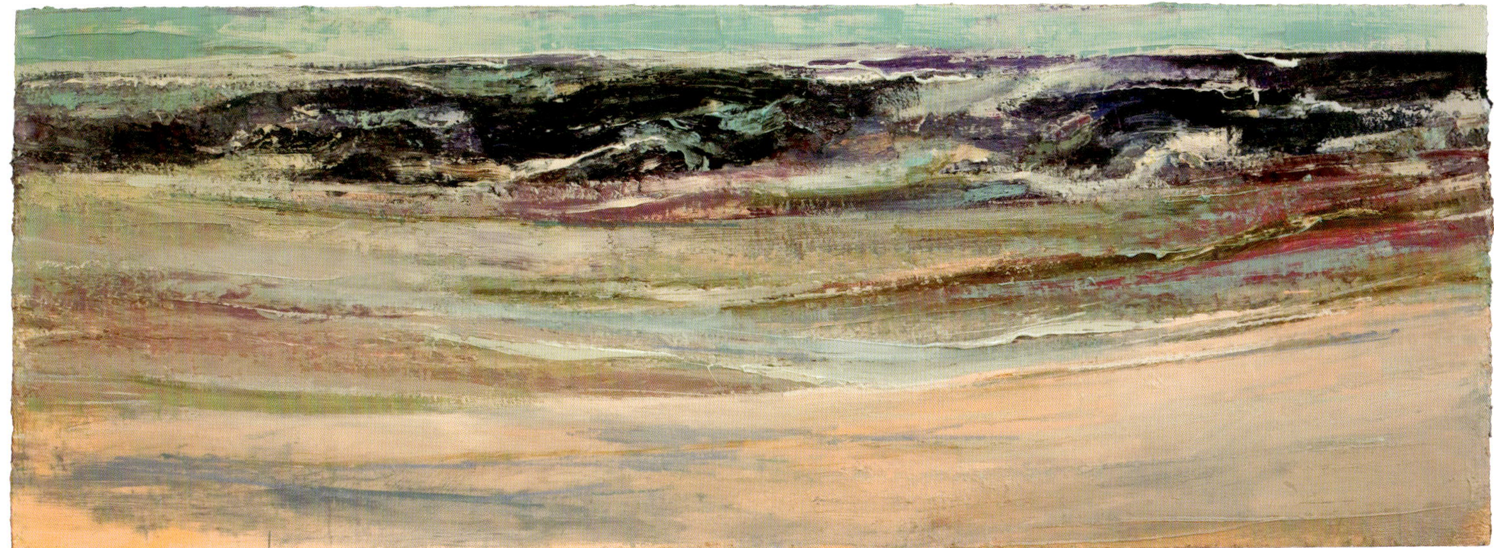

Fig. 27
Barry Gealt
Prince Edward Island, 2009
Oil on panel
Collection of Ann and Rusty Harrison

Fig. 28
Barry Gealt
Distant Waterfall, 2001
Oil on panel
Collection of Ann and Rusty Harrison

Waterfall (fig. 30), mossy rocks protrude among gushing, twisting water surfaces in a bas-relief. "It's like he lifted something from nature and stuck it in your house," the painting's owner, Tony Moravec, declared.[35]

Barry Gealt has enriched and nurtured colleagues, students, and collectors alike. As Matthew Ballou wrote,

> Regardless of how anyone may feel about his subject matter, Barry Gealt the *painter* is inescapable, and the density of his surfaces and absolute no-holds-barred approach to the physical act of making paintings are undeniable. His achievements as a teacher and a painter are inextricably tied to his belief in image-making as a way of life. . . . [He is] a man who has been able to keep investing in others for fifty years while at the same time finding a way to hold tightly to home and studio, diligently creating works that really do embody something of his characteristic force and grace, directness and nuance, speed and depth."[36]

Gealt's staggering output of artwork, with solo exhibitions since the 1970s and semiannual one-man shows throughout this century, evince his commitment to his art. For this project, at age seventy, Gealt has explored his interior consciousness to discover what experiences and personal artistic discoveries continue to drive his work. This indomitable search for an authentic, singular voice is motivated by his stalwart belief that music, art, and writing are the ultimate expressions of the human soul. His landscapes embody a great paradox: they are timeless, important works of art that are uniquely of our own tumultuous time.

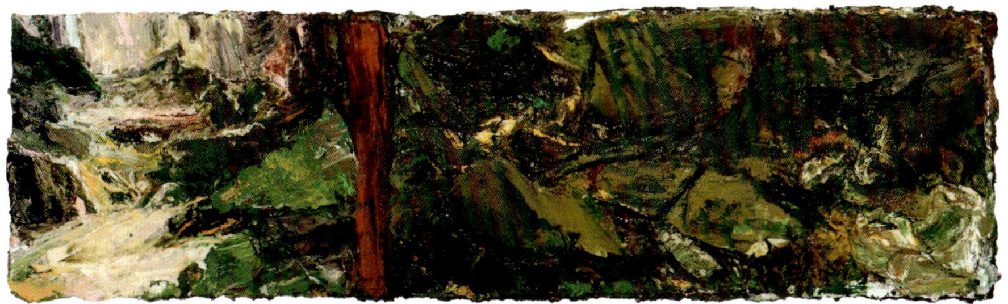

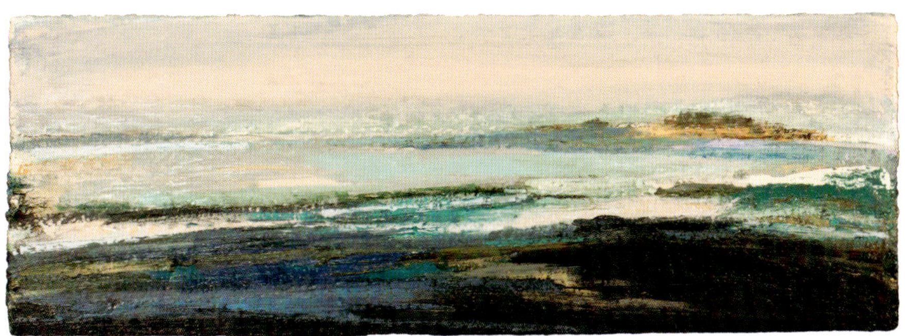

Fig. 29
Barry Gealt
Low Tide, Outer Bar Island, 8:30 am, 2010, Corea, Maine, 2010–11
Oil on panel
Courtesy Galerie Beaux-arts des Amériques, Montréal

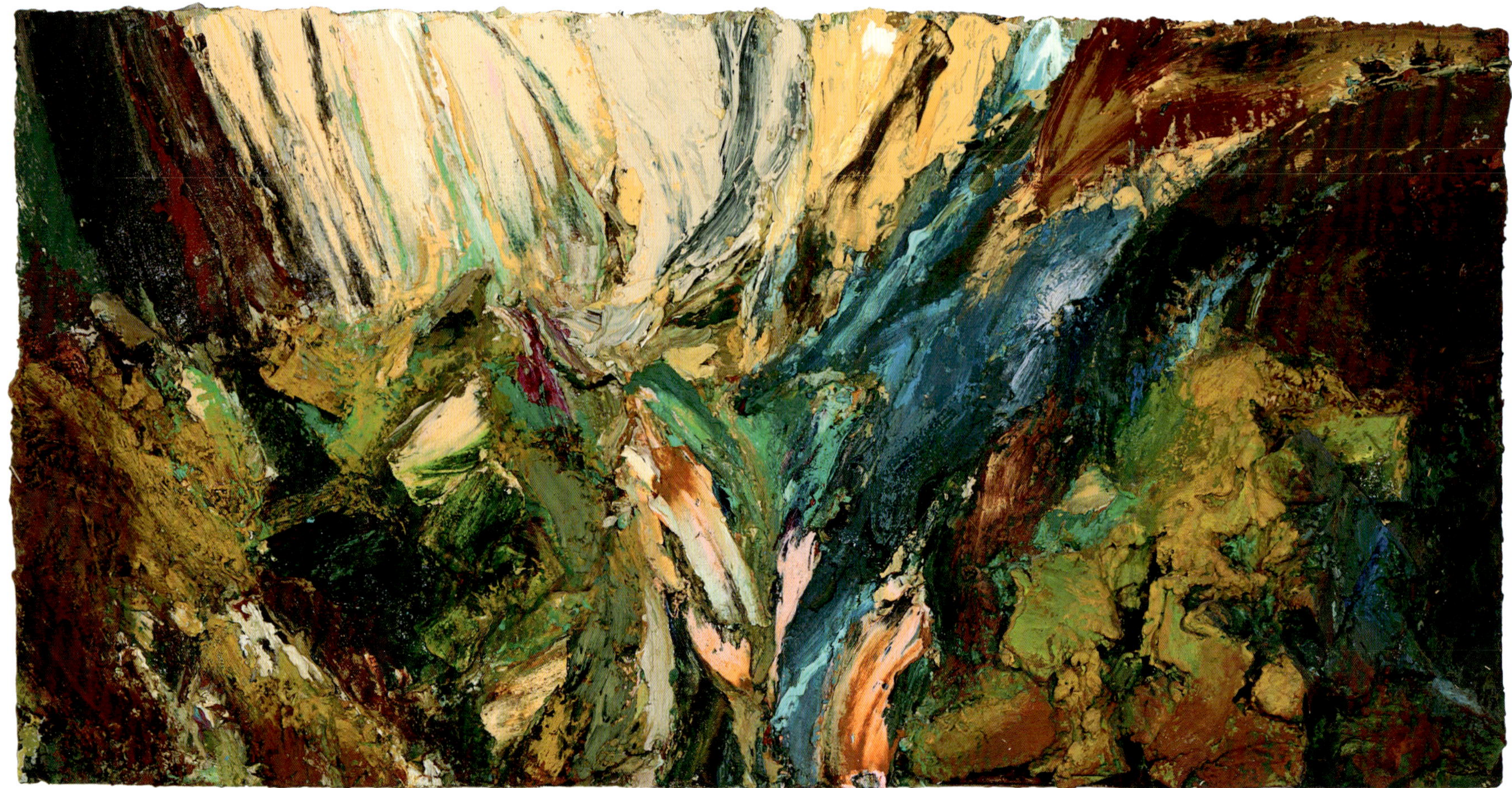

Fig. 30
Barry Gealt
Raging Waterfall, 2006
Oil on panel
Collection of Anthony J. Moravec
Columbus, Indiana

Endnotes

1 Interview with Barry Gealt in his studio, Spencer, IN, February 4, 2011
2 Interview with Barry Gealt at Hob Nob restaurant, Nashville, IN, June 10, 2011
3 Ibid.
4 Correspondence from Barry Gealt to Rachel Perry, January 22, 2012
5 Ibid.
6 Interview with Barry Gealt at IU Art Museum, Bloomington, IN, April 11, 2011
7 Interview with Barry Gealt at IU Art Museum, Bloomington, IN, April 11, 2011
8 Ibid.
9 Interview with Barry Gealt, trip to Attica, IN, October 20, 2011
10 Interview with Barry Gealt in his studio, Spencer, IN, February 4, 2011
11 Faunce, Sarah, and Nochlin, Linda, *Courbet Reconsidered,* Yale University Press, 1988, p. 7
12 "Gealt on Teaching," written comments by Barry Gealt, no date
13 Letter from Matthew Ballou to Rachel Perry, August 6, 2011
14 Ibid.
15 Ibid.
16 Letter from Christine Mugnulo to Rachel Perry, August 9, 2011
17 Letter from Karrie Maxwell to Rachel Perry, August 29, 2011
18 Letter from Rachel Welling to Rachel Perry, September 7, 2011
19 "Gealt on Teaching," written comments by Barry Gealt, no date
20 Powell, Richard R., *Wabi Sabi Simple,* Adams Media, 2004.
21 Interview with Barry Gealt, Hob Nob restaurant, Nashville, IN, June 10, 2011
22 Interview with Barry Gealt, trip to Zionsville, IN, May 31, 2011
23 Notes for Barry Gealt lecture, no date
24 Interview with Barry Gealt in his studio, Spencer, IN, February 4, 2011
25 Ibid.
26 Ibid.
27 Barry Gealt, quoted in *Etretat* (gallery brochure), Collins...QC, March 2007 at Collins, Lefebvre, Stoneberger Beaux-arts des Ameriques, Montreal, QC, March, 2007
28 Interview with Barry Gealt in his studio, Spencer, IN, February 4, 2011
29 Quote in Piurek, Ryan, "Canvases of Change," *Indiana University Research & Creative Activity* on-line magazine, Vol. 27, Number 2, Spring 2005.
30 Interview with Barry Gealt in his studio, Spencer, IN, February 4, 2011
31 Ibid.
32 Grayford, Martin, and Wright, Karen, editors, *The Grove Book of Art Writing,* Grove/Atlantic, Inc. New York, 1998, p. 41.
33 Interview with Barry Gealt in his studio, Spencer, IN, February 4, 2011
34 Barry Gealt quote in essay by Lucienne Lefebvre Glaubinger, in *Barry Gealt* (gallery brochure), Beaux-arts des Ameriques, Montreal, QC, April, 2011.
35 Interview with Barry Gealt at Tony Moravec residence, Columbus, IN, May 5, 2011
36 Letter from Matthew Ballou to Rachel Perry, August 6, 2011

Catalogue

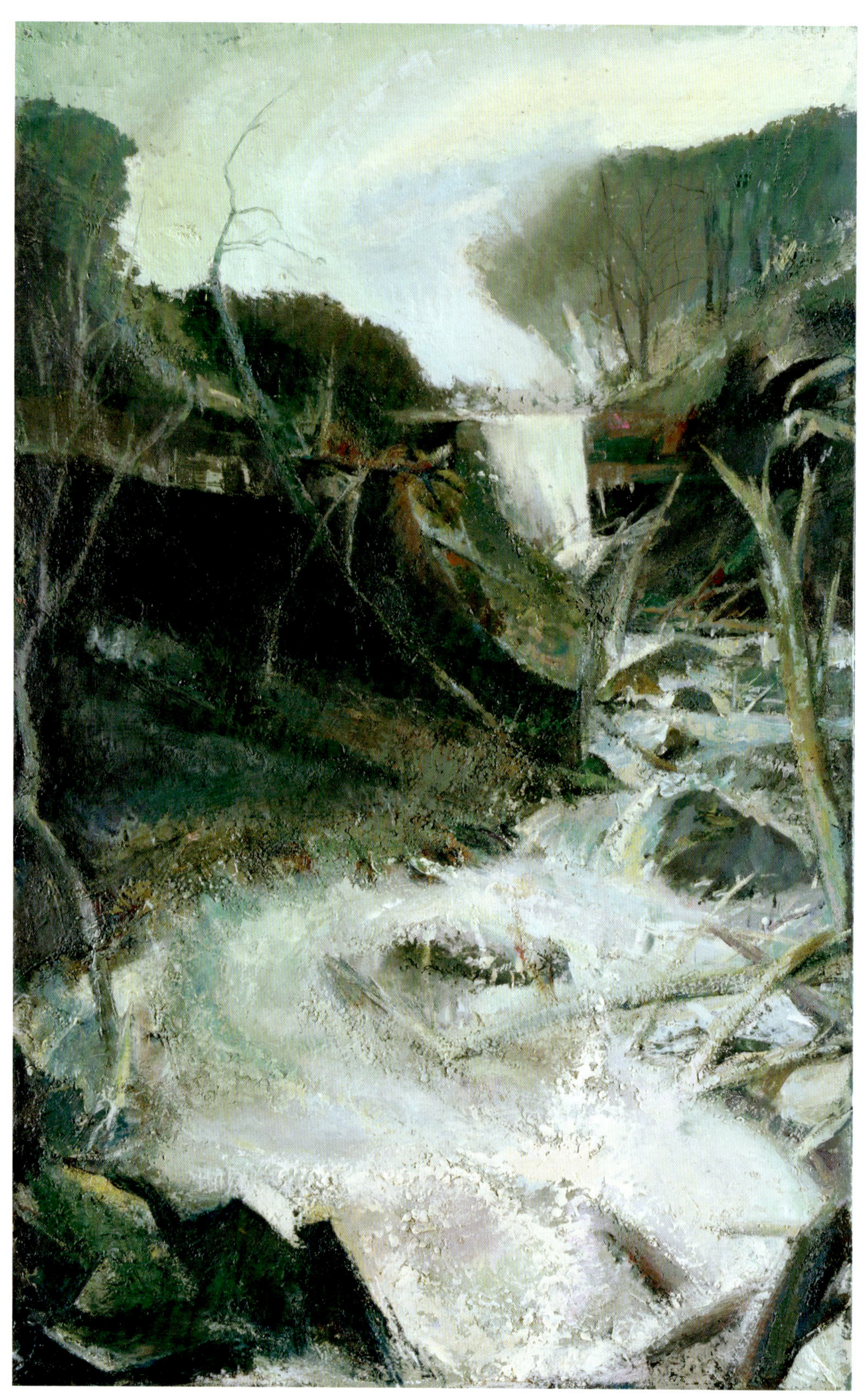

After the Storm, 1987–88
Oil on canvas
62″ x 40″
Collection of Faegre Baker Daniels, LLP,
Indianapolis
[not in exhibition]

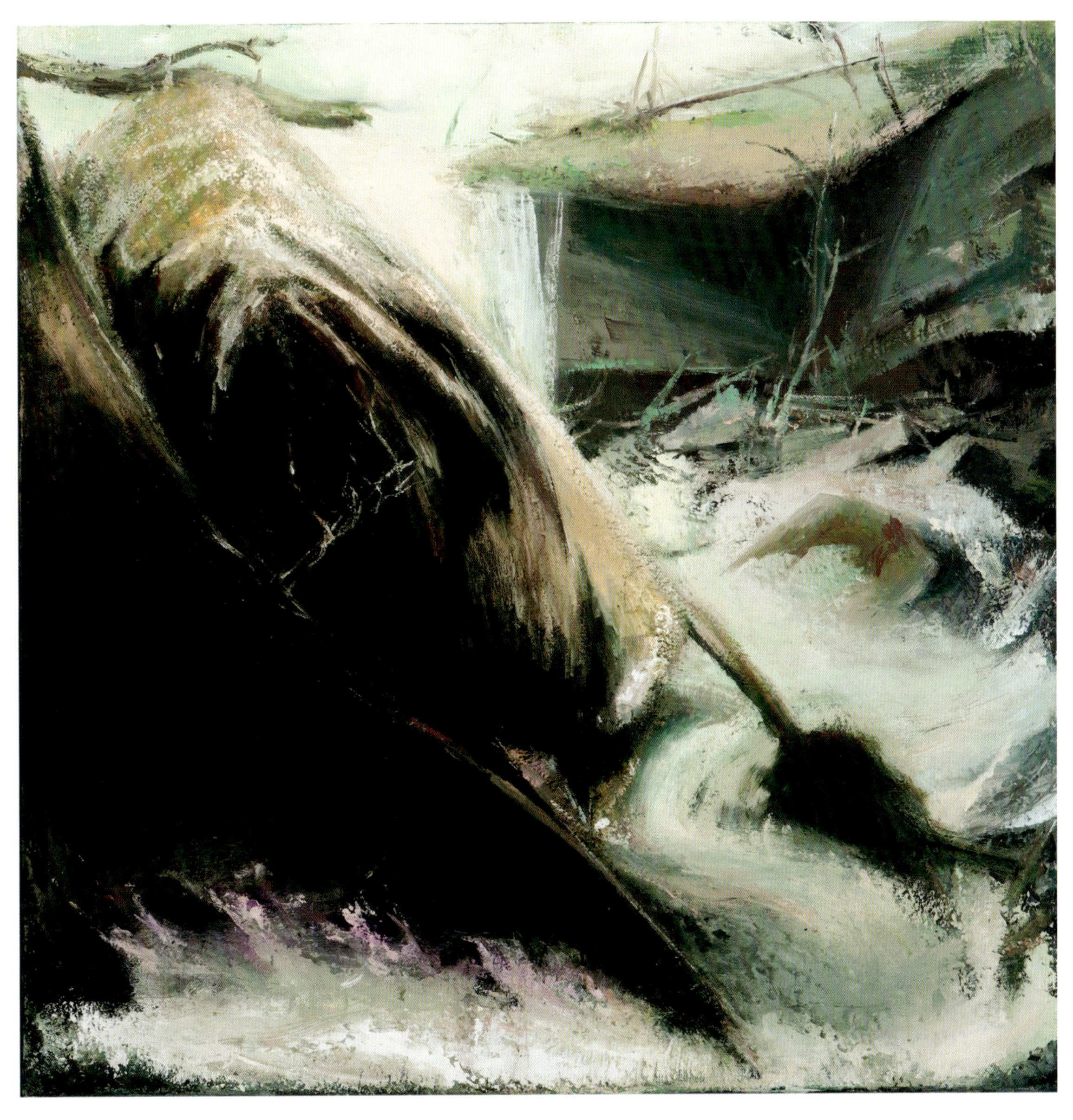

November, 1988–89
Oil on canvas
30″ x 30″
Collection of Bob and Suzanne Mann

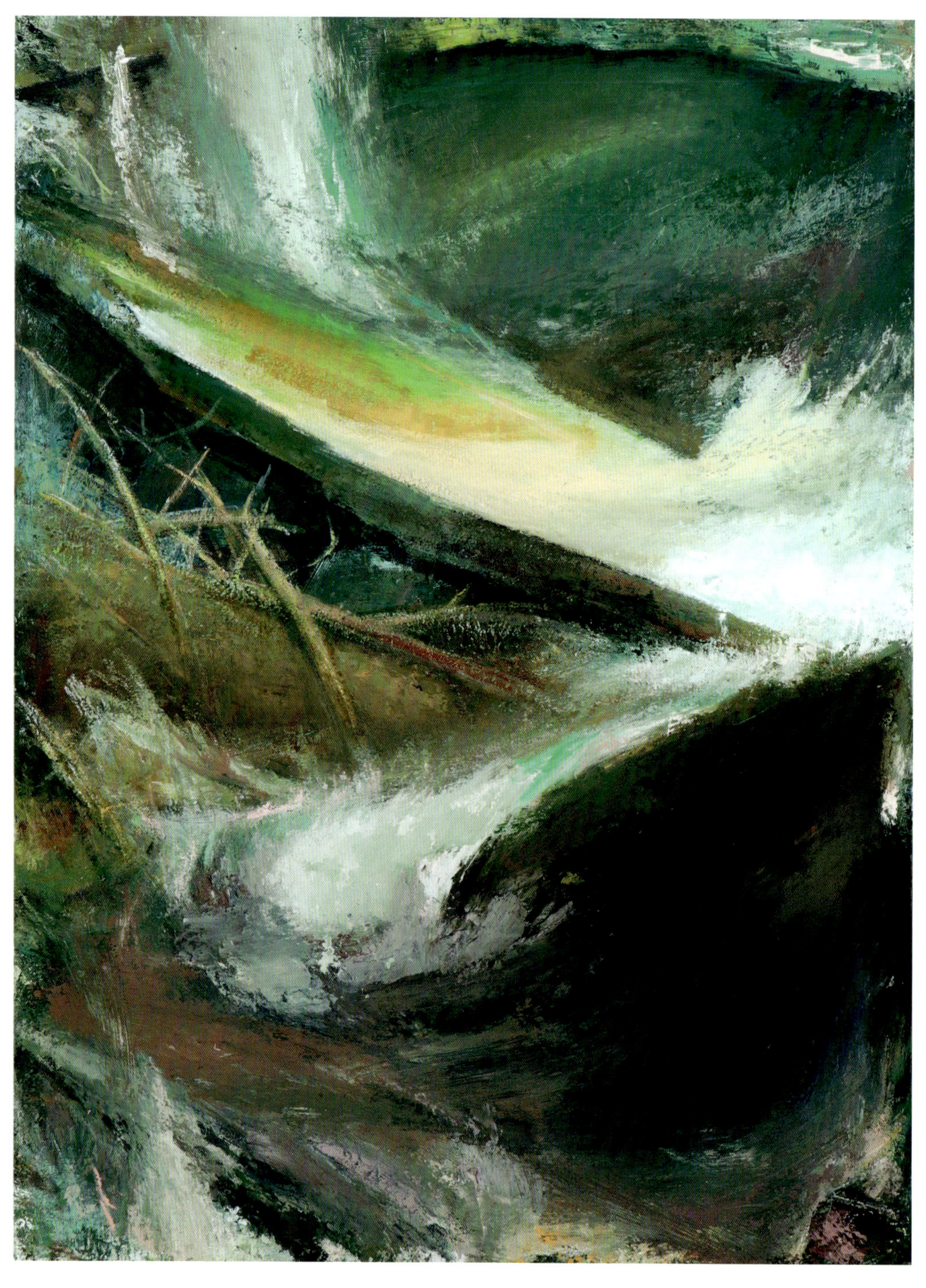

Sliding Rocks, Brittle Cold, 1988–89
Oil on canvas
47" x 34 ¾"
Collection of Lisa McKee Lanham and
Michael W. Halstead

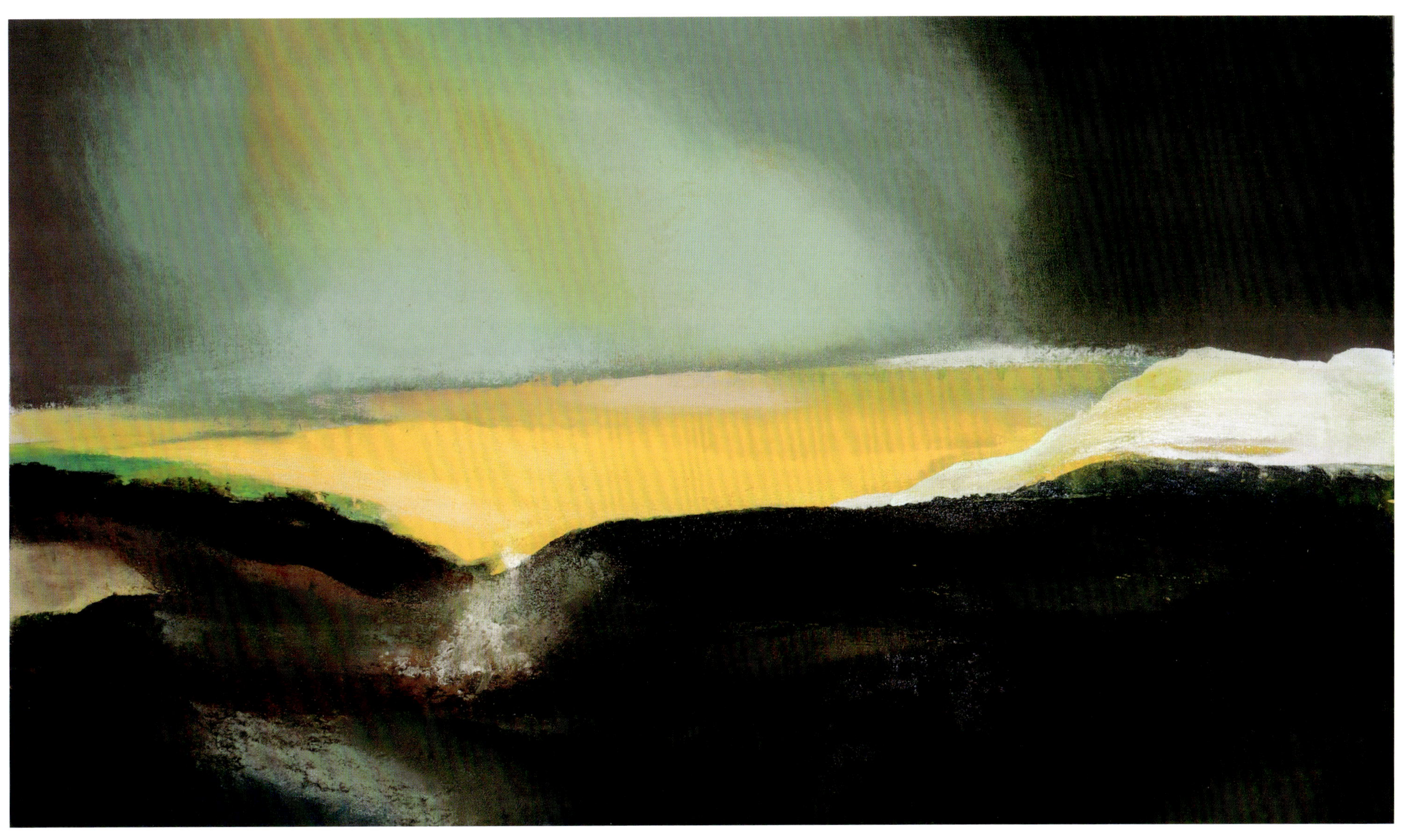

Owen County Vista, 1994
Oil on canvas
39″ x 69″
Collection of the Office of the President, IU

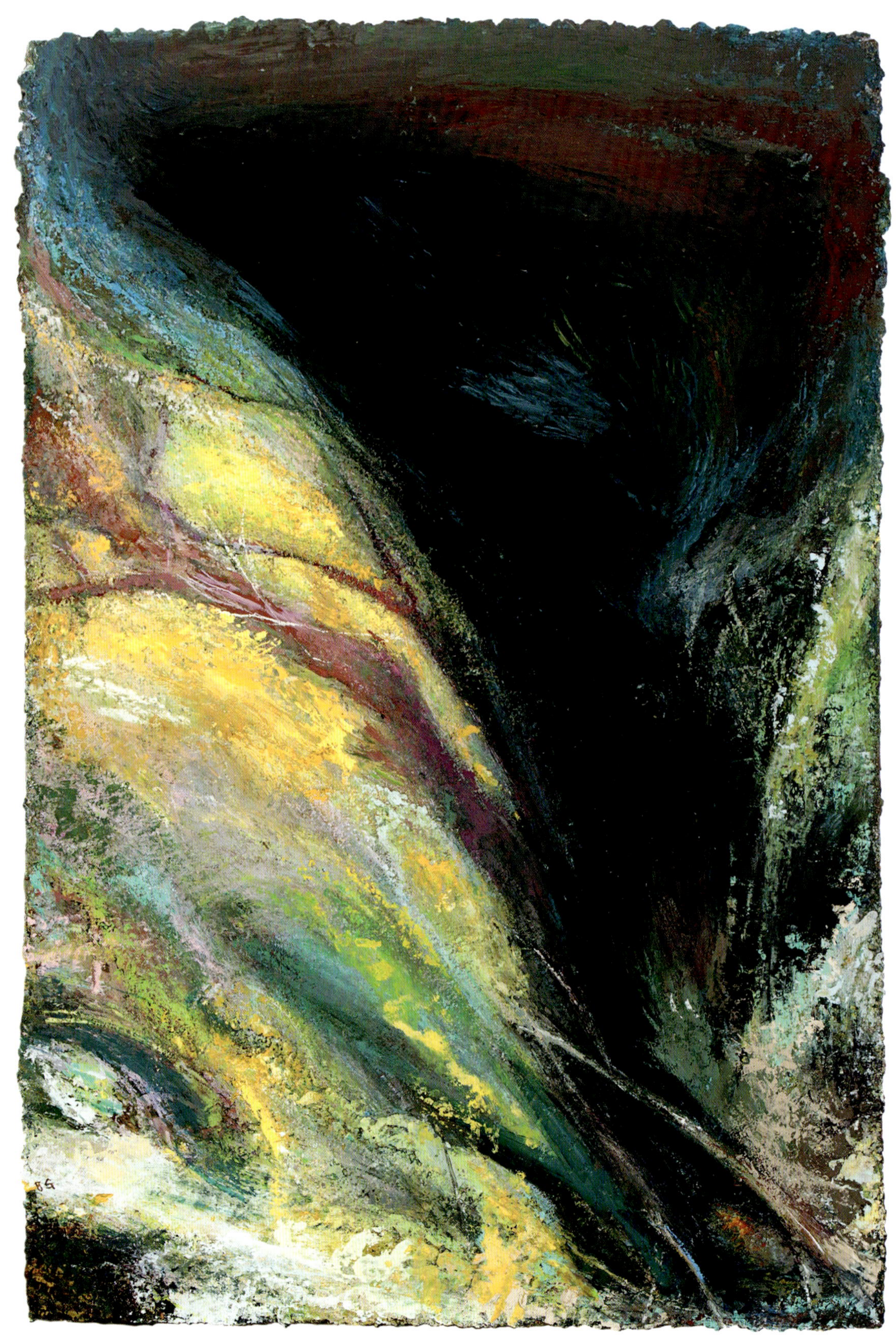

The Cave, 1994
Oil on canvas
62″ x 40″
Collection of Anthony J. Moravec
Columbus, Indiana

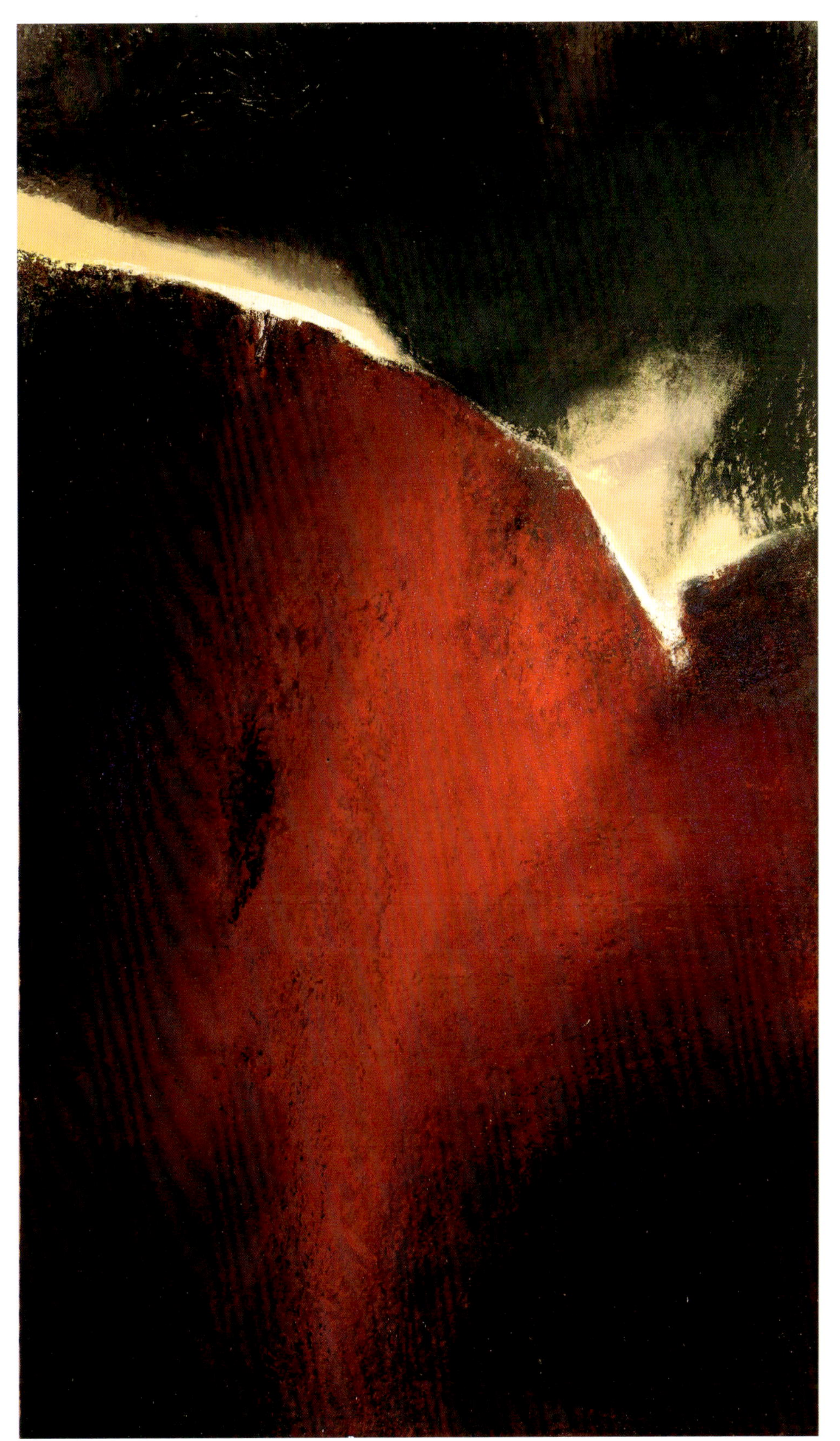

The Reddening Glow of Night, 1994
Oil on canvas
72 ¼″ x 42 ¼″
Collection of Thies Knauf, Shelbyville

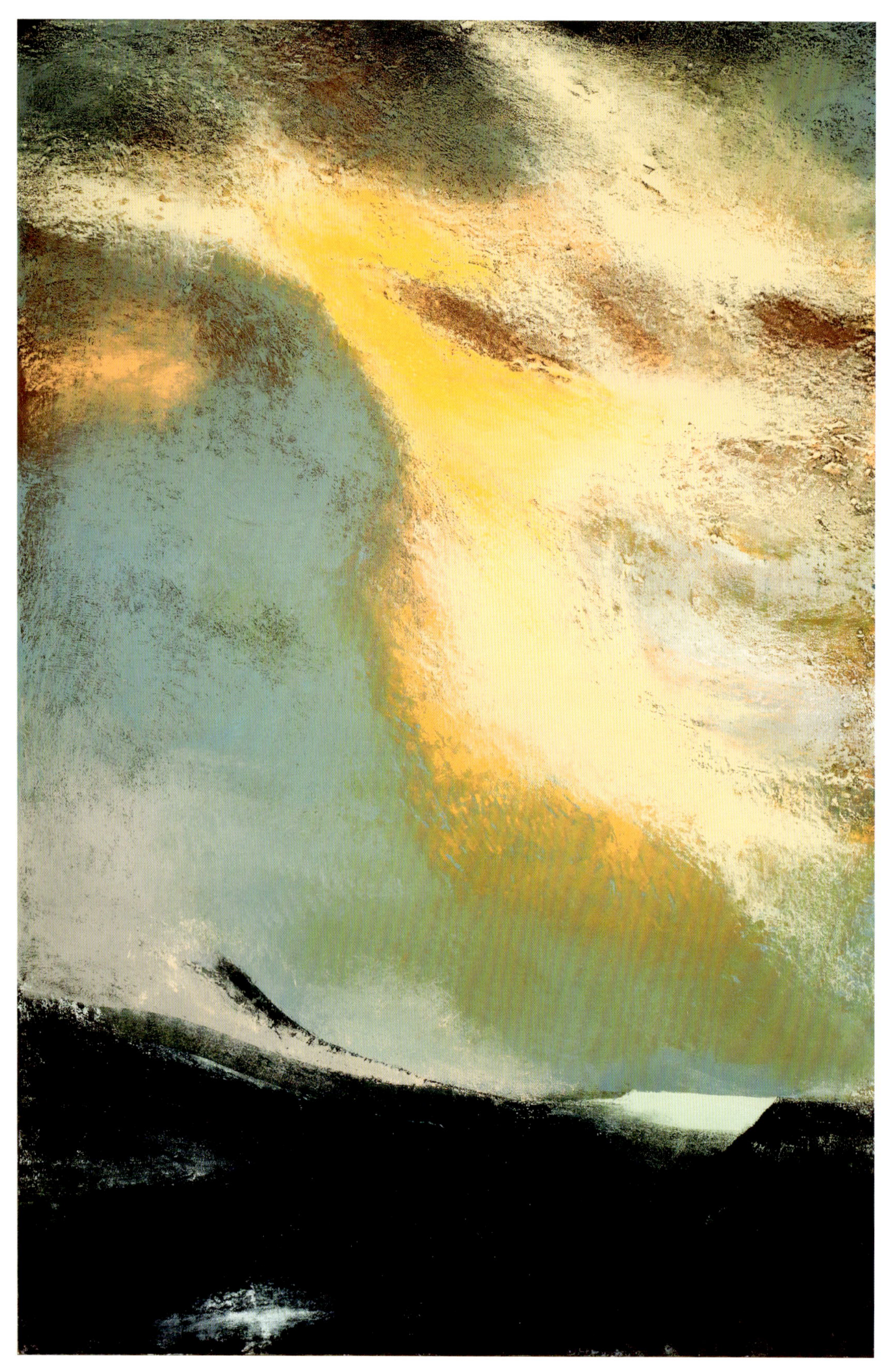

Fleeting Clouds, 1994
Oil on canvas
72″ x 48″
Collection of Thies Knauf,
Shelbyville

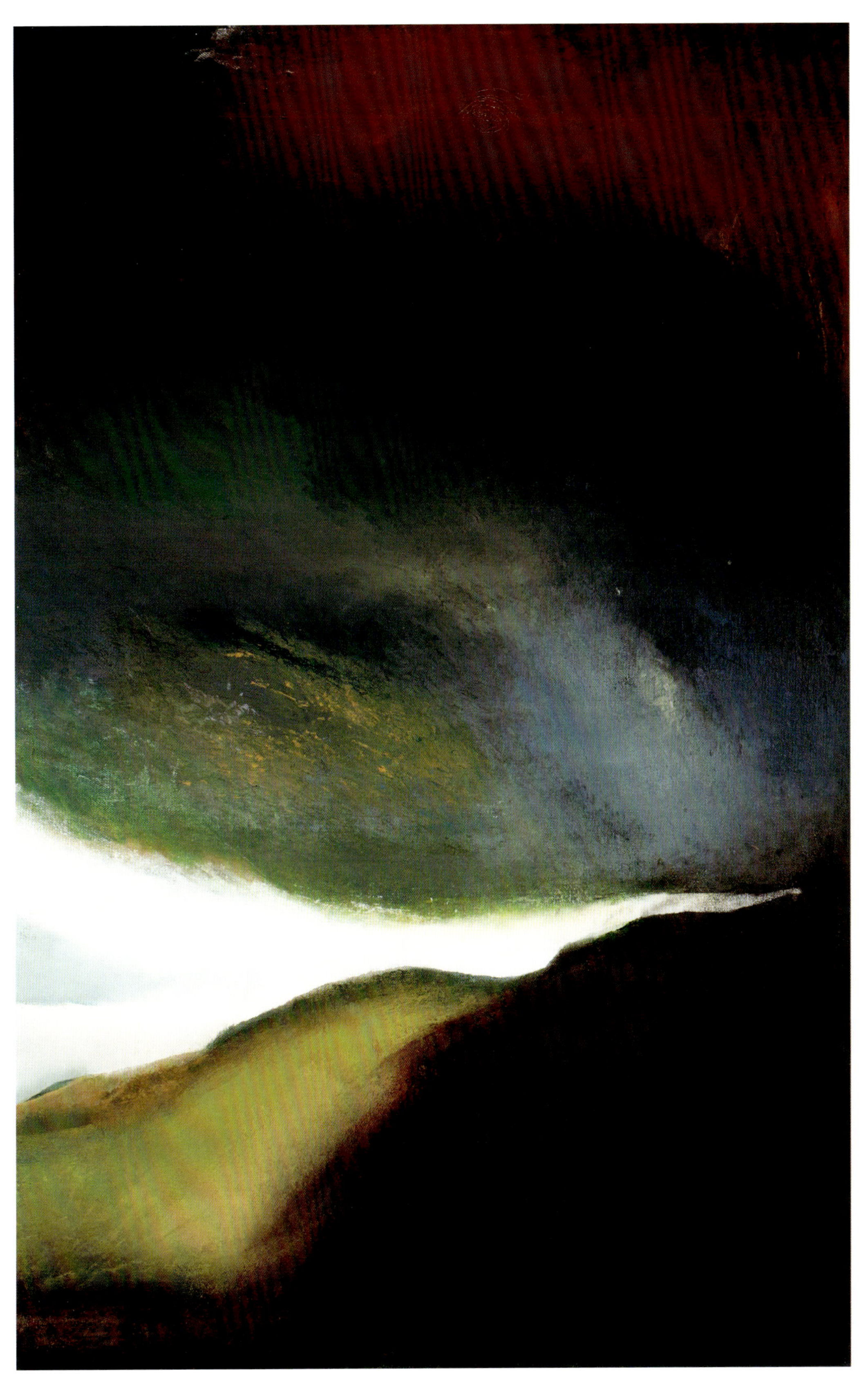

Before the Storm, 1994
Oil on canvas
66″ x 42 ¼″
Collection of Linda Baden and
Charles Cole

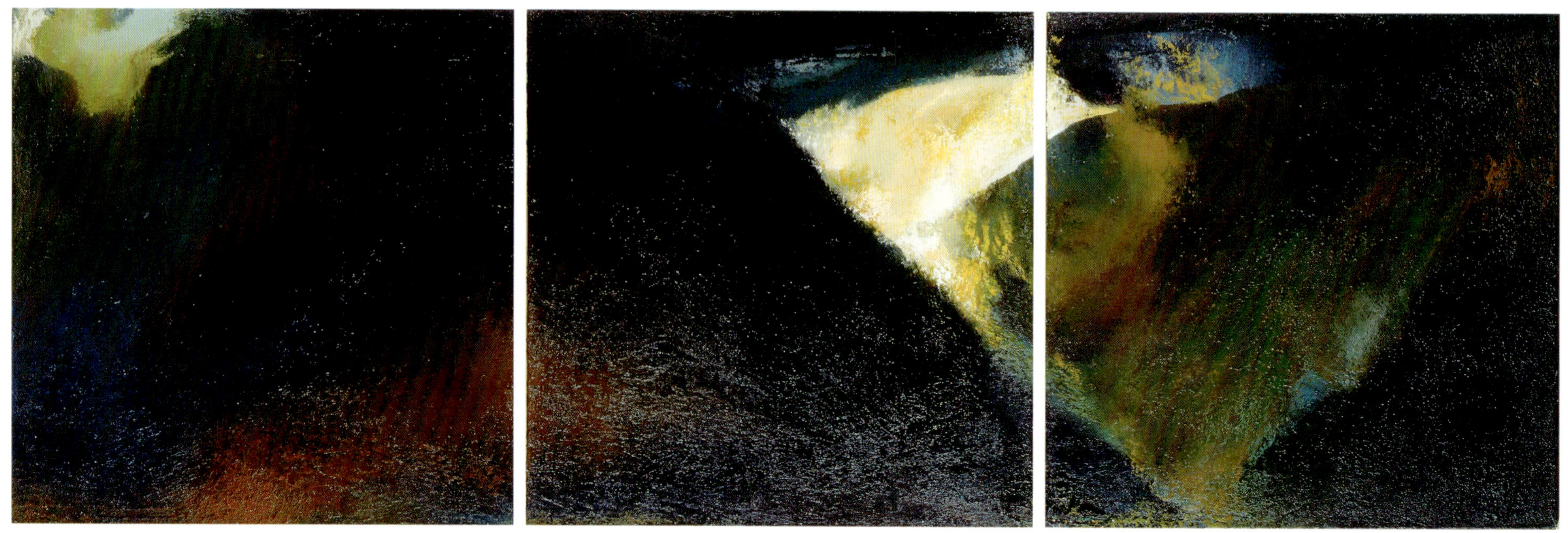

Indiana Hills, 1994
Oil on canvas
Triptych: each panel, 36″ x 36″
Collection of Dorit and Gerald Paul
[not in exhibition]

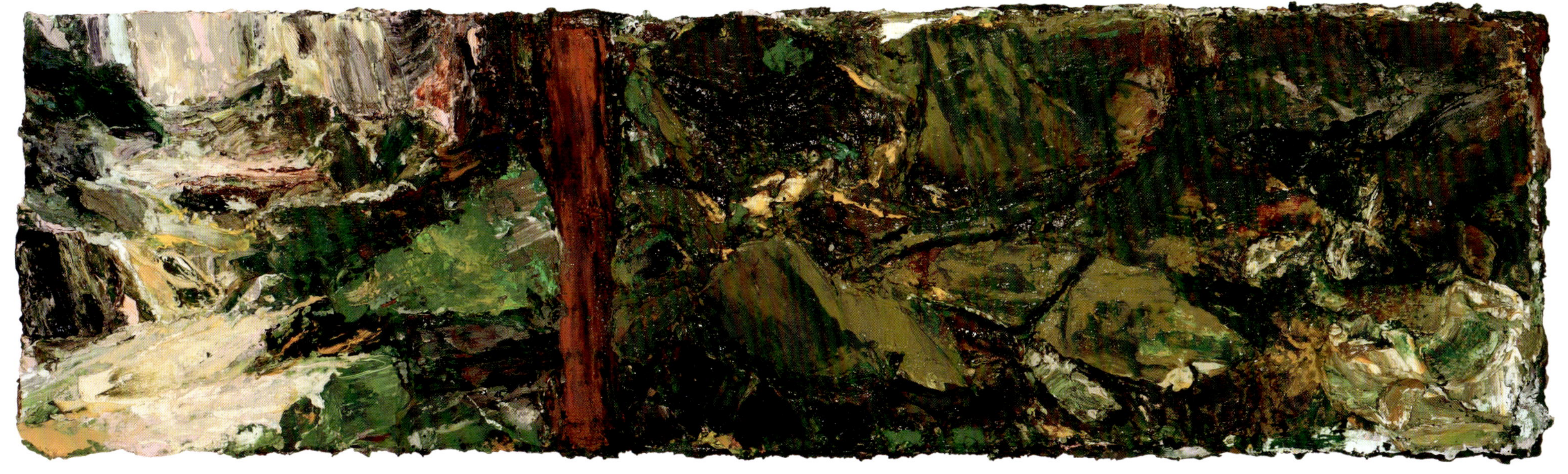

Distant Waterfall, 2001
Oil on canvas
14″ x 50 ½″
Collection of Ann and Rusty Harrison

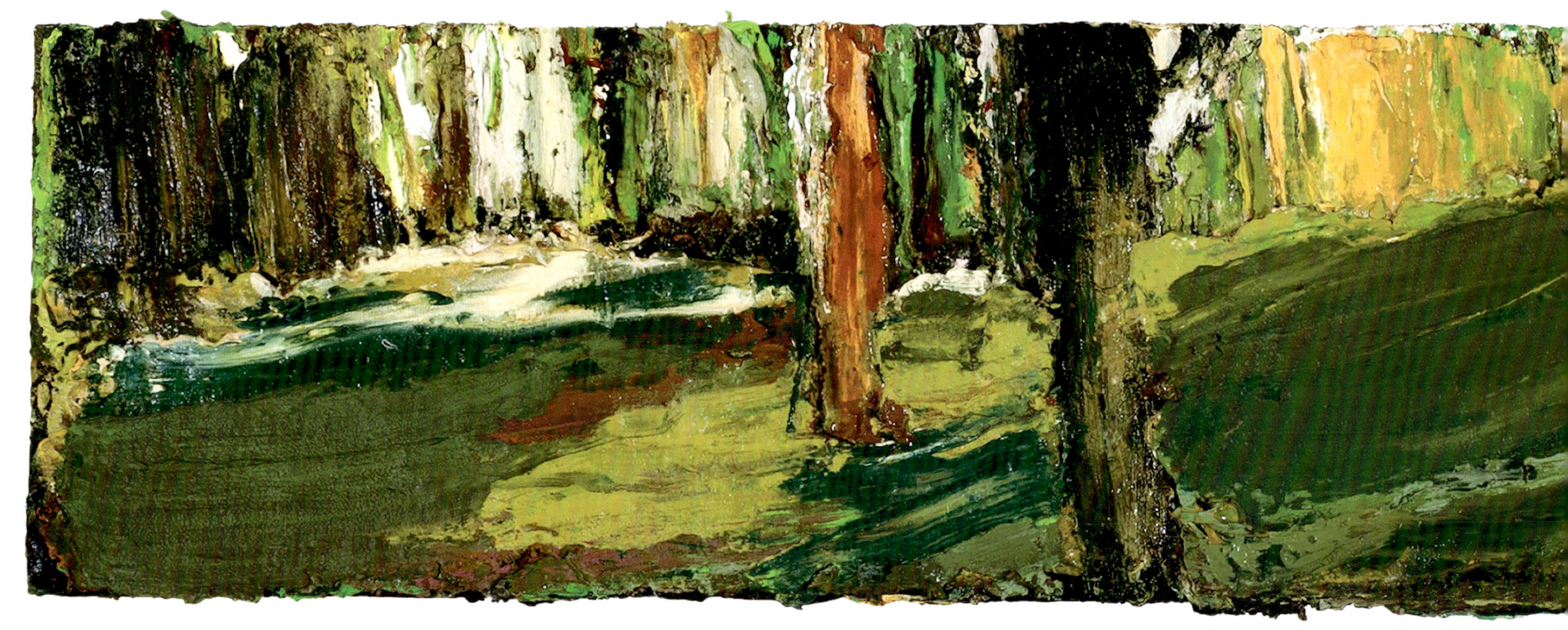

In the Heart of the Woods, 2002
Oil on canvas
10 ¼″ x 57 ⅜″
Collection of Amanda and Andrea Ciccarelli,
Bloomington

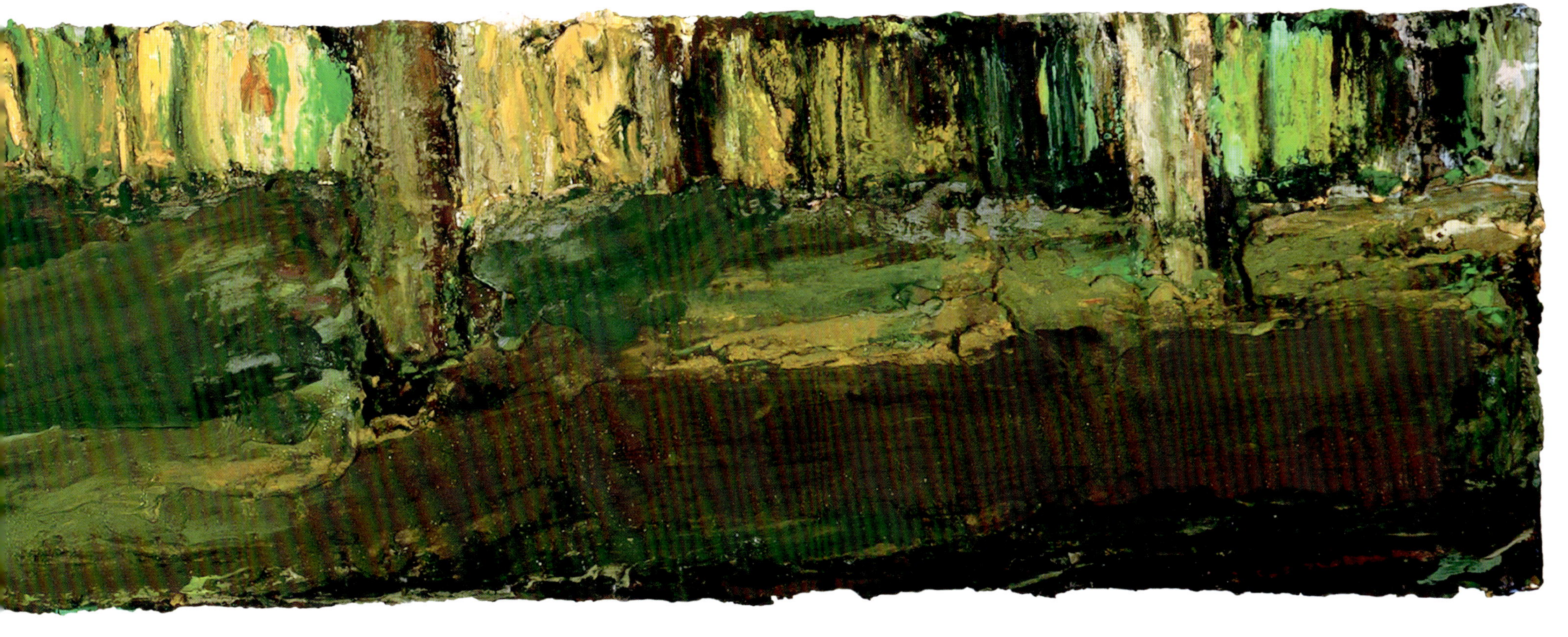

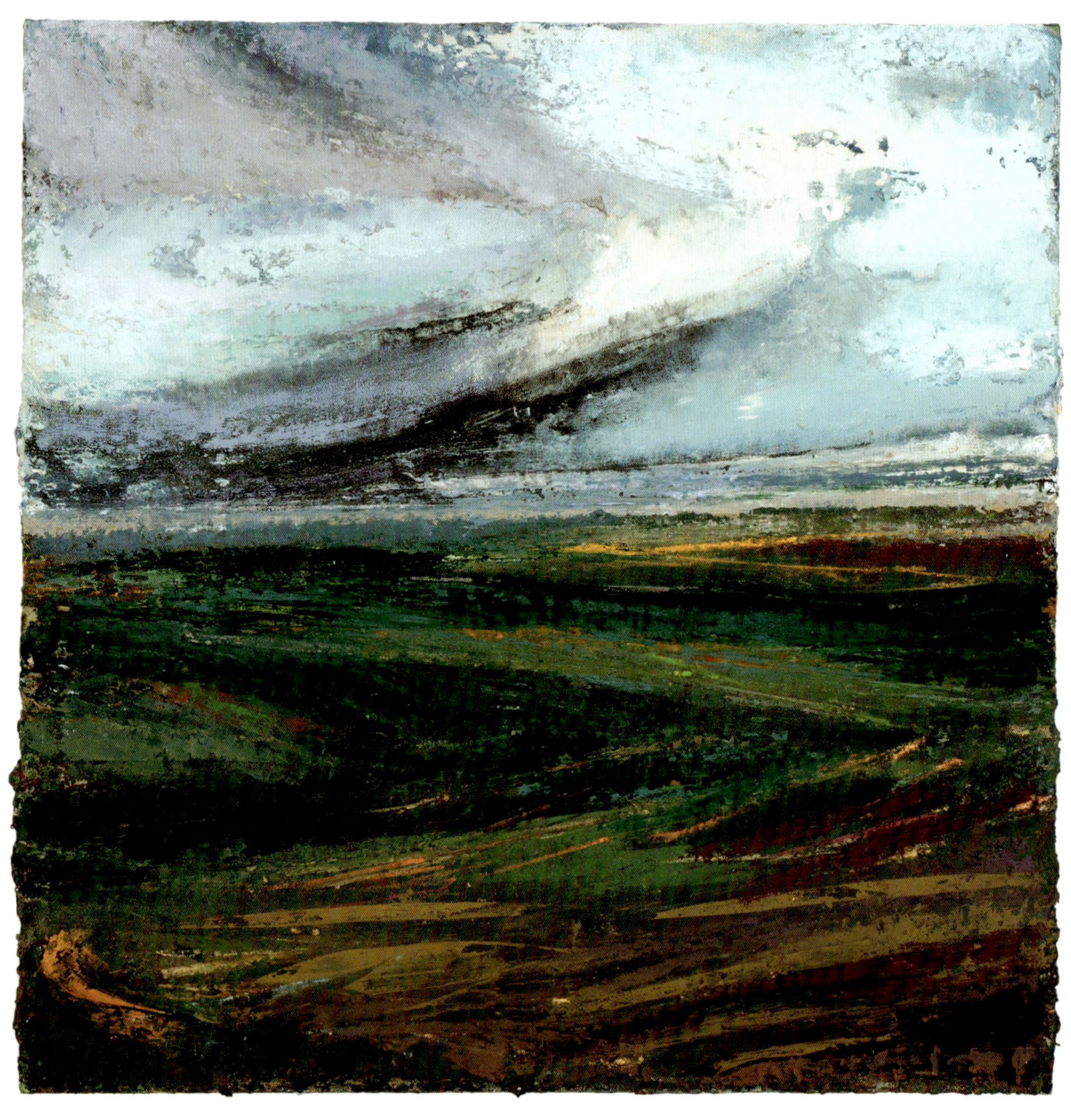

Indiana Vista, 2001
Oil on canvas
36″ x 36″
Collection of Ann and Rusty Harrison

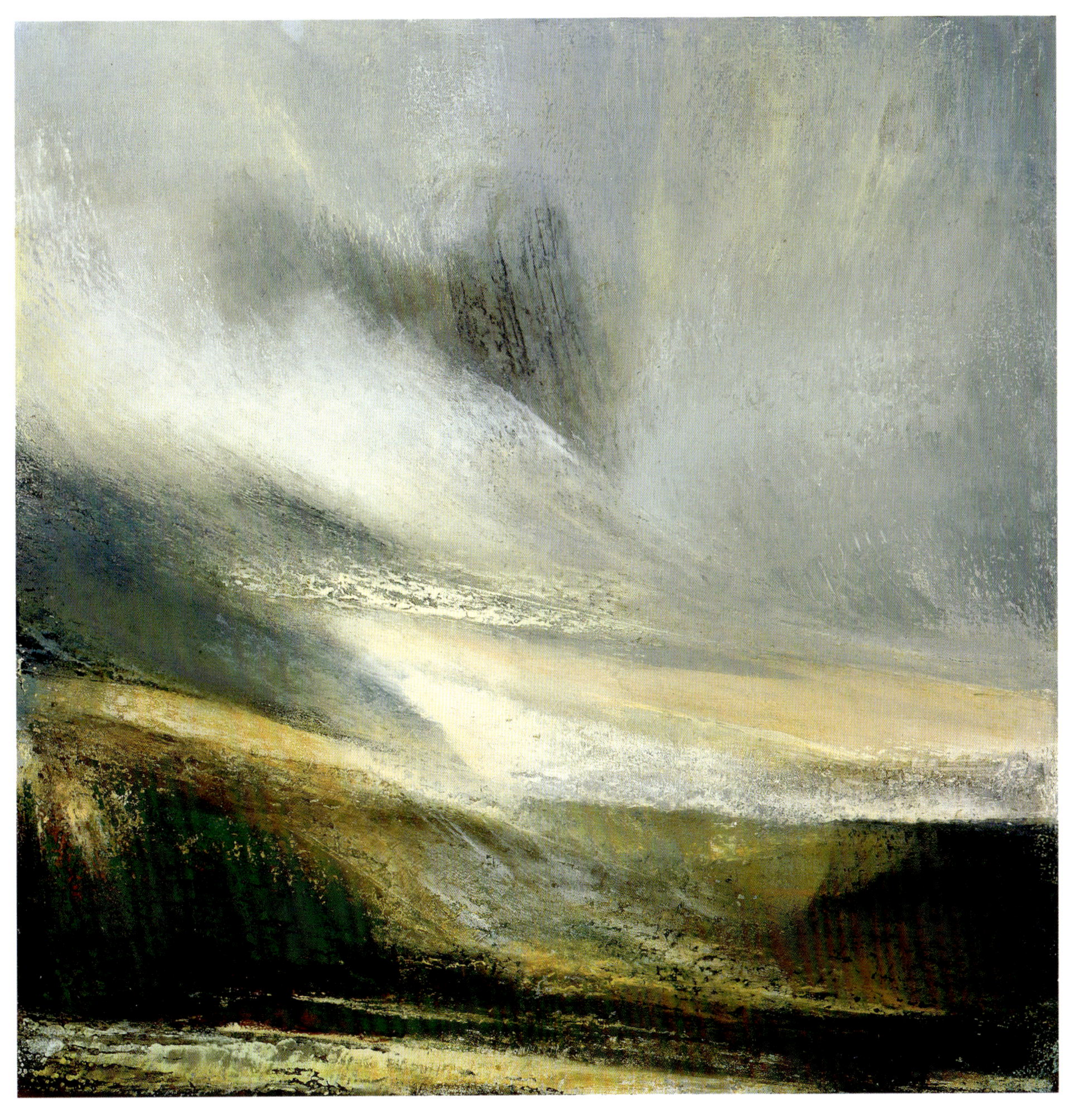

Evening Light, 2001
Oil on panel
42" X 42"
Private collection, Cologne, Germany
[not in exhibition]

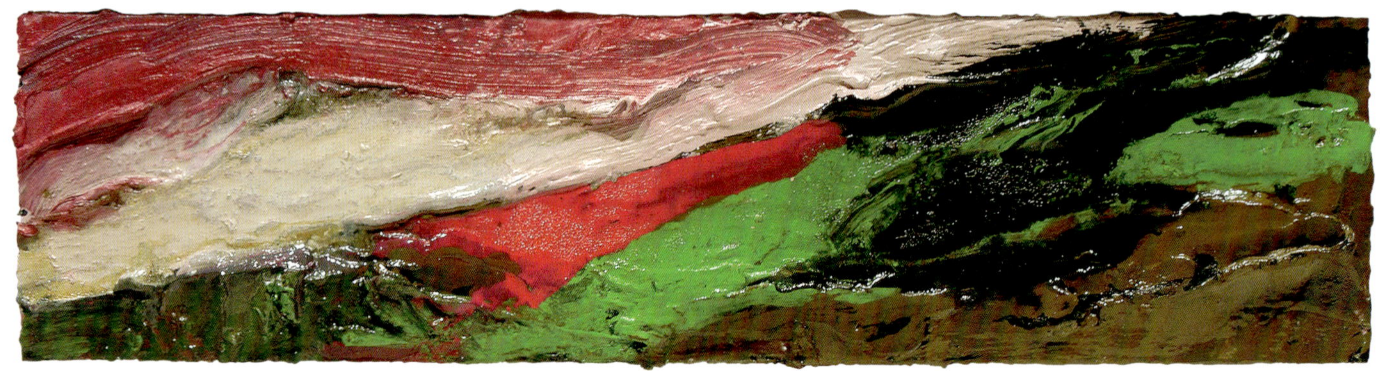

Paradise Valley, Utah, 2005
Oil on panel
10" X 21"
Private collection of Gabriele and Dieter Bamberger,
Cologne, Germany
[not in exhibition]

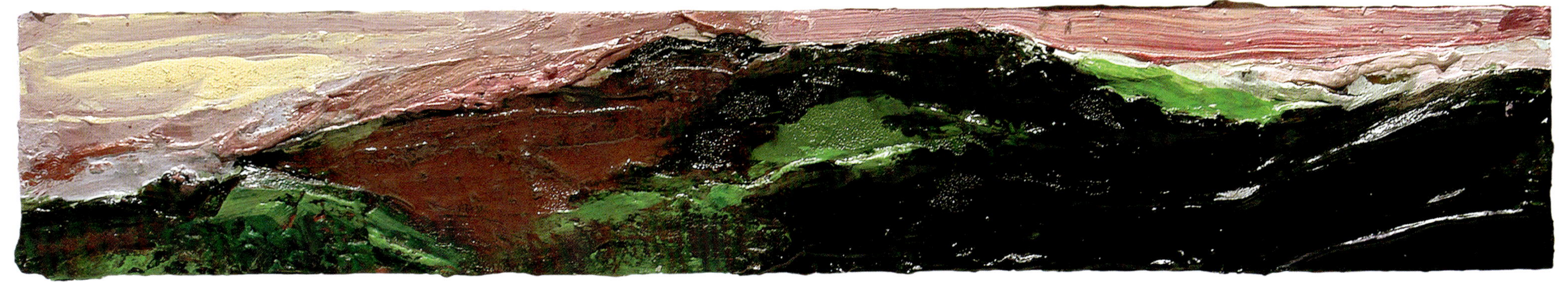

Paradise Valley, Utah, 2005
Oil on panel
10″ X 41½″
Private collection of Gabriele and Dieter Bamberger,
Cologne, Germany
[not in exhibition]

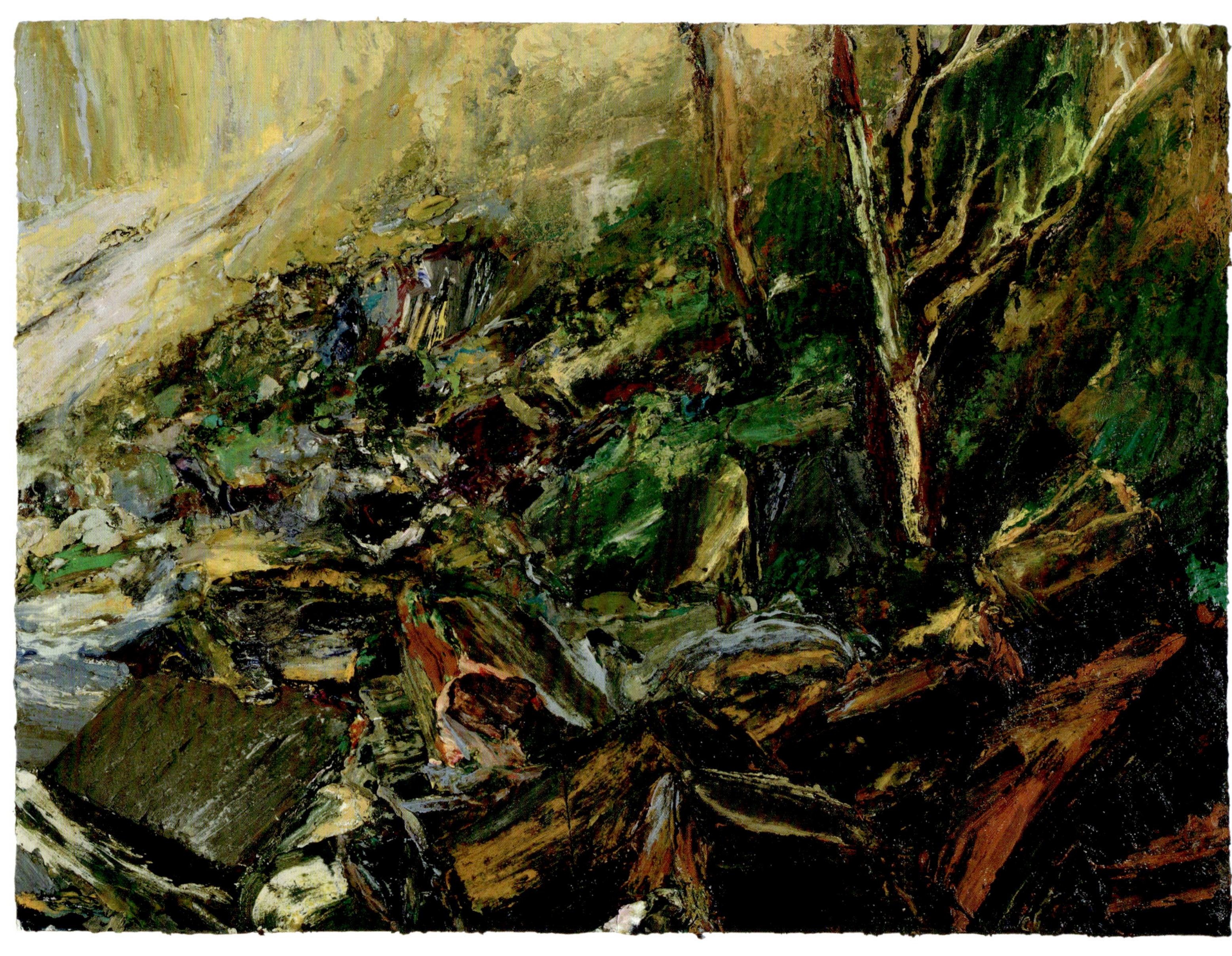

Low Wooded Hill, 2003
Oil on panel
30″ x 40″
Private collection, Indianapolis
[not in exhibition]

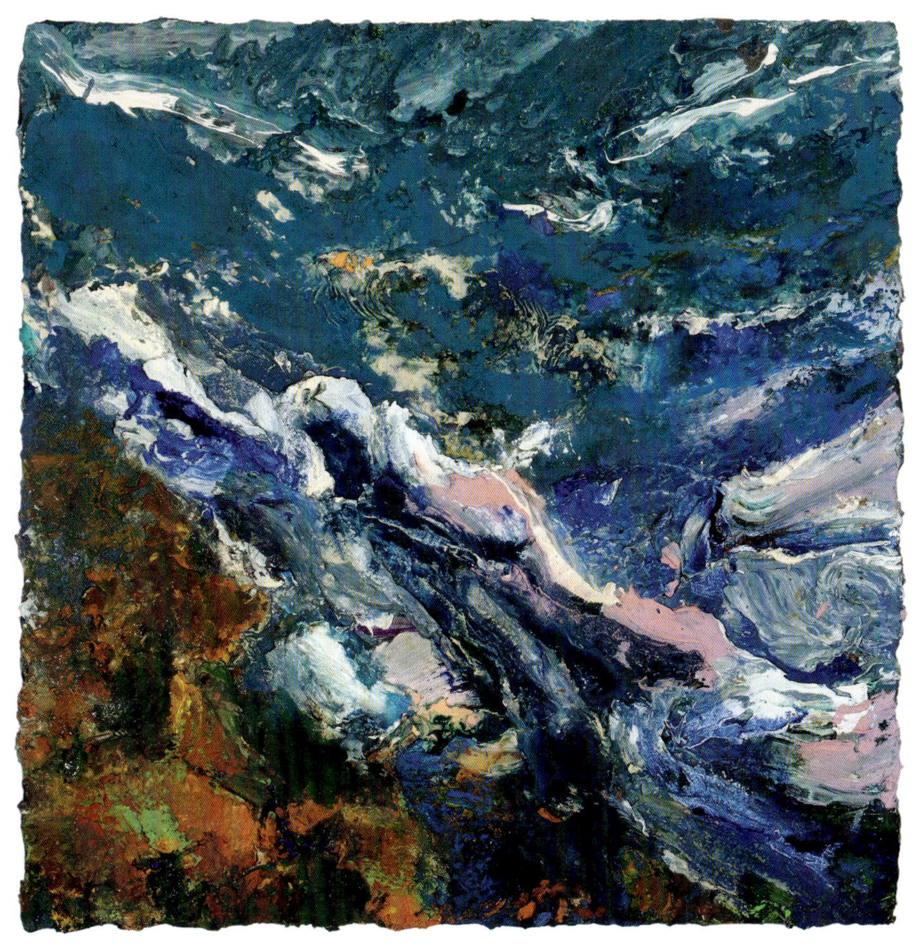

Dieppe Waves, 2005
Oil on panel
22″ x 22″
Private collection

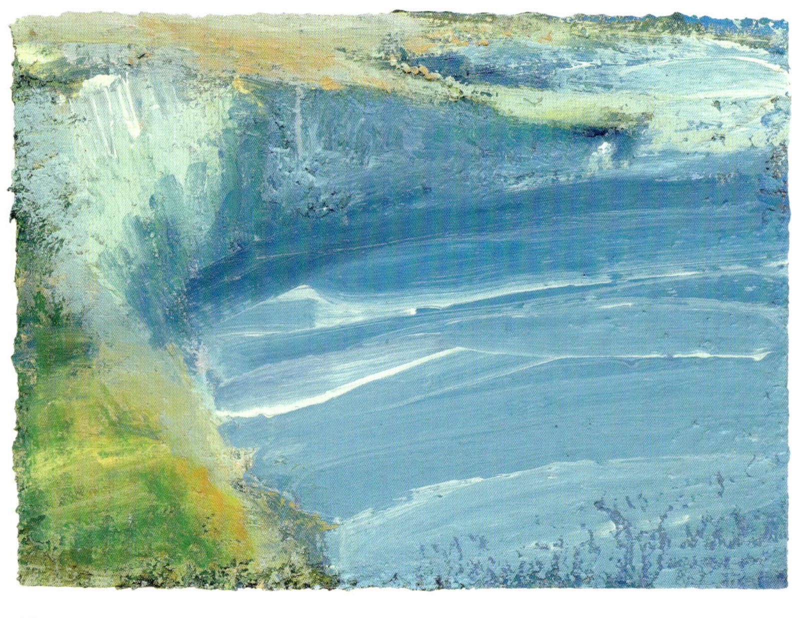

V

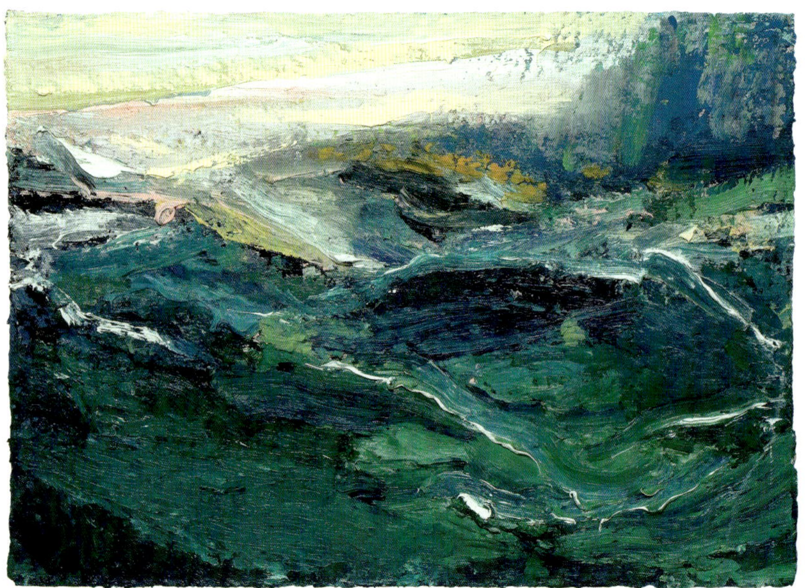

IV

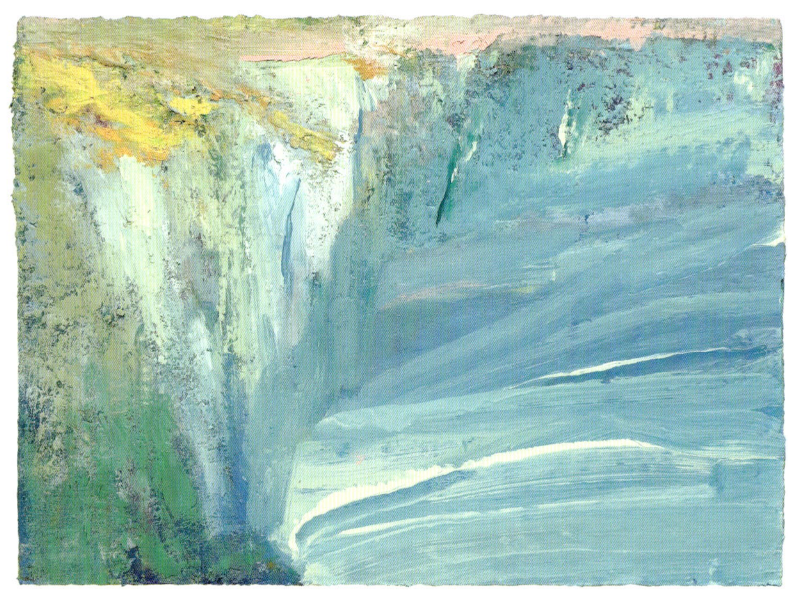

III

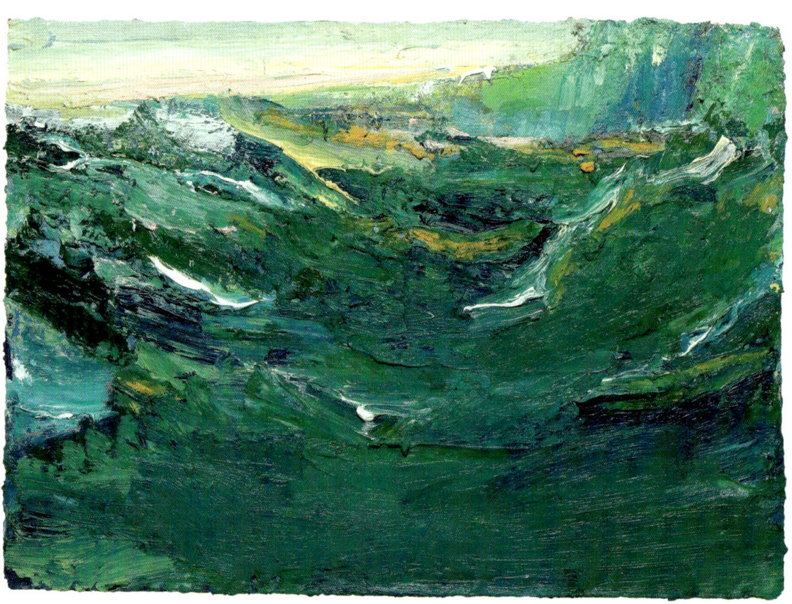

II

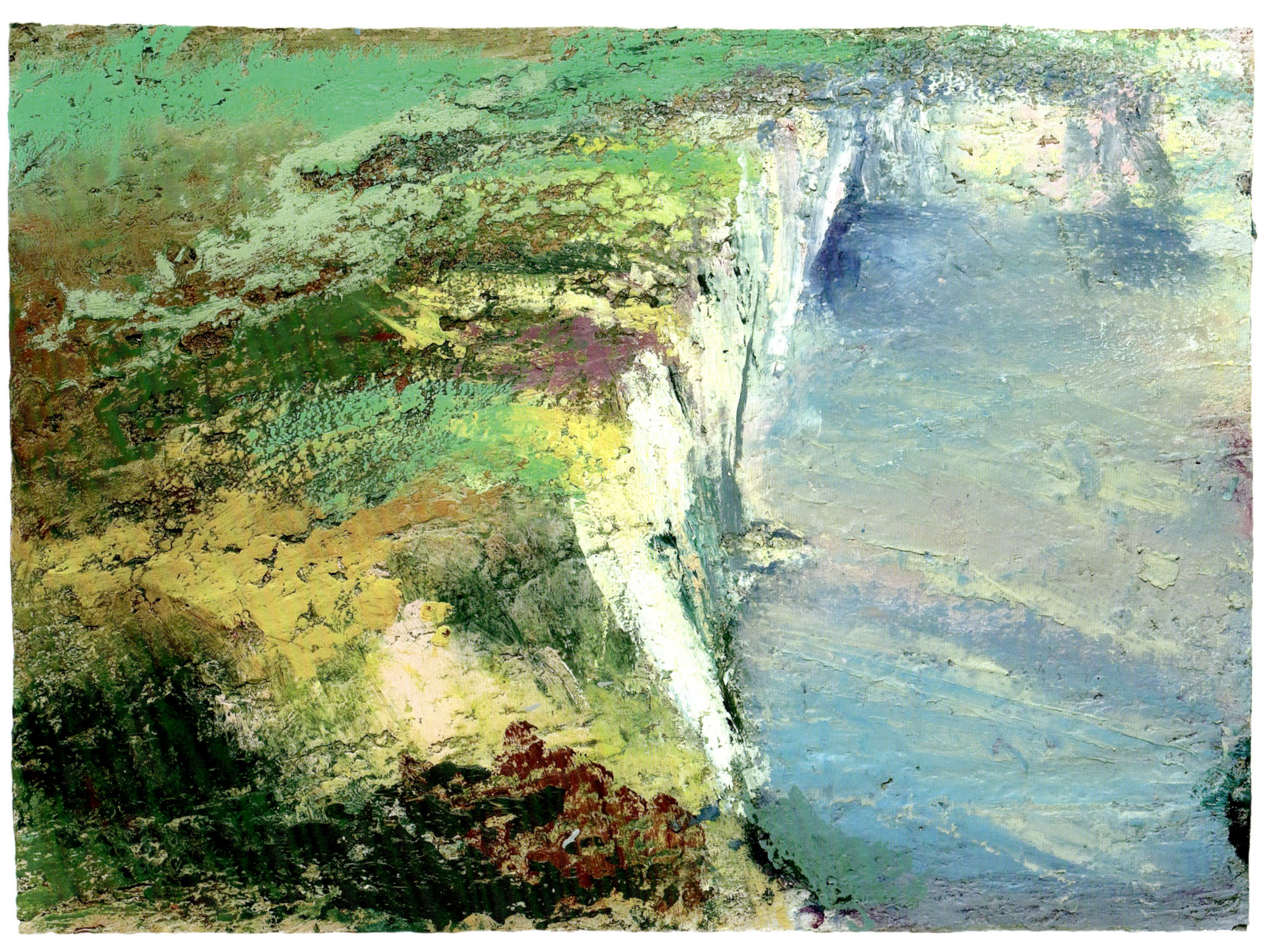

I

Etretat I–V, 2007
Oil on canvas
22″ x 28″
Collection of Ann and Rusty Harrison

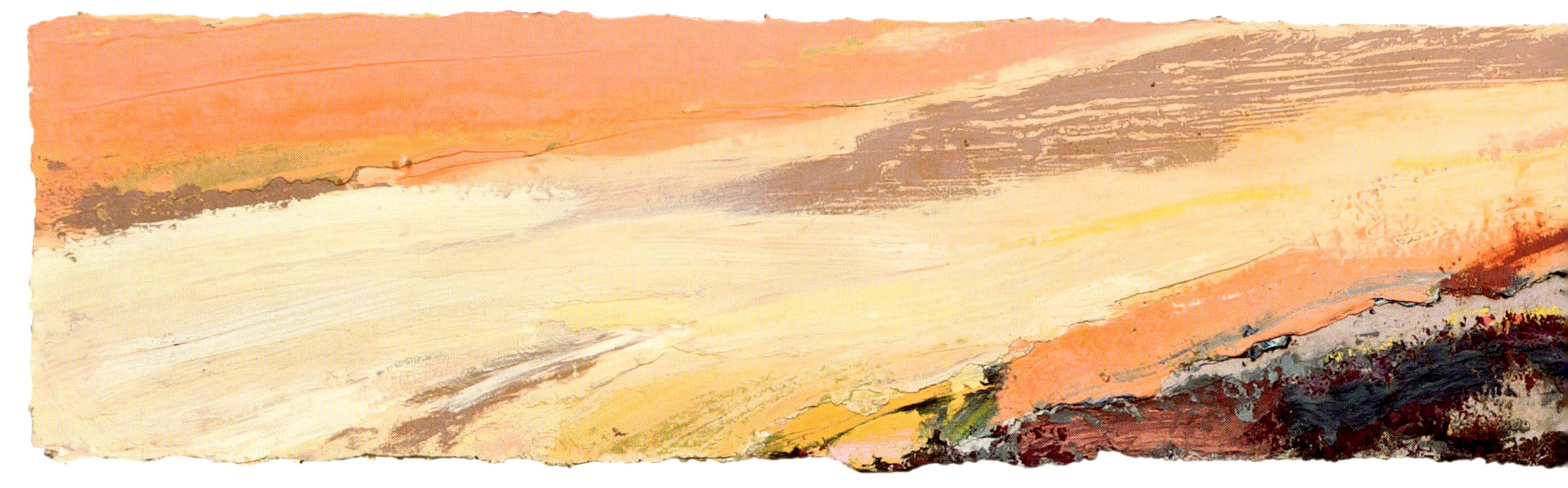

Early Evening Sunset, 2007
Oil on panel
11″ x 83″
Collection of Frank and Frances Kelly, Zionsville

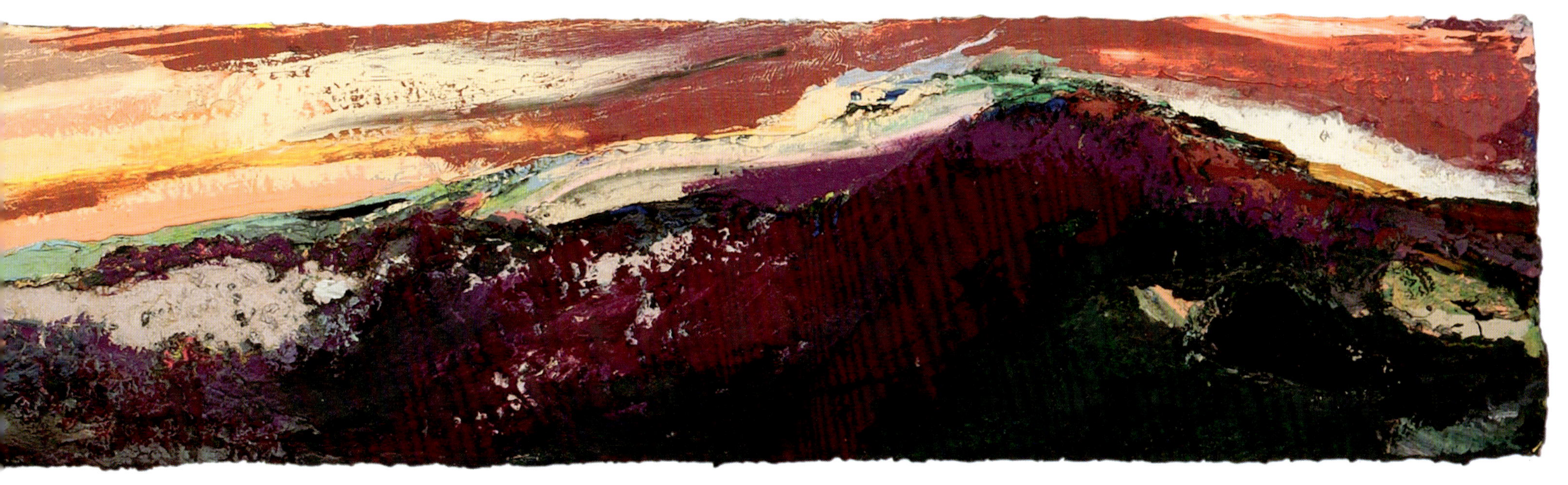

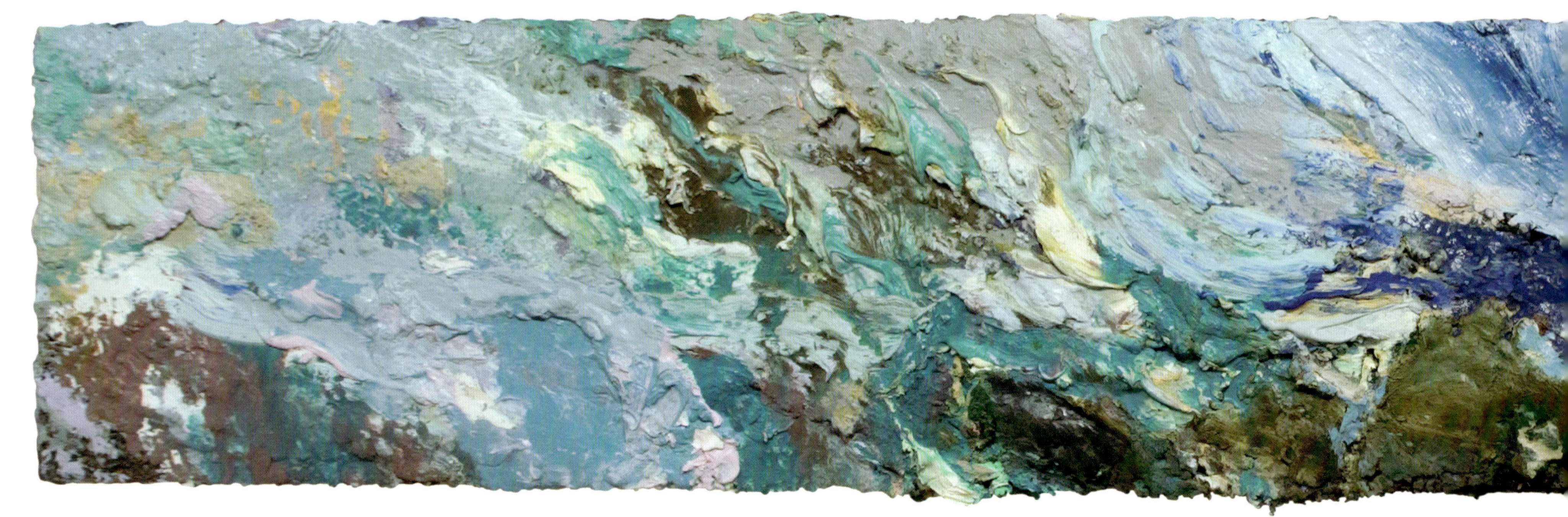

Barfleur, 2007
Oil on panel
13 ¼″ x 84″
Collection of Anthony J. Moravec,
Columbus, Indiana

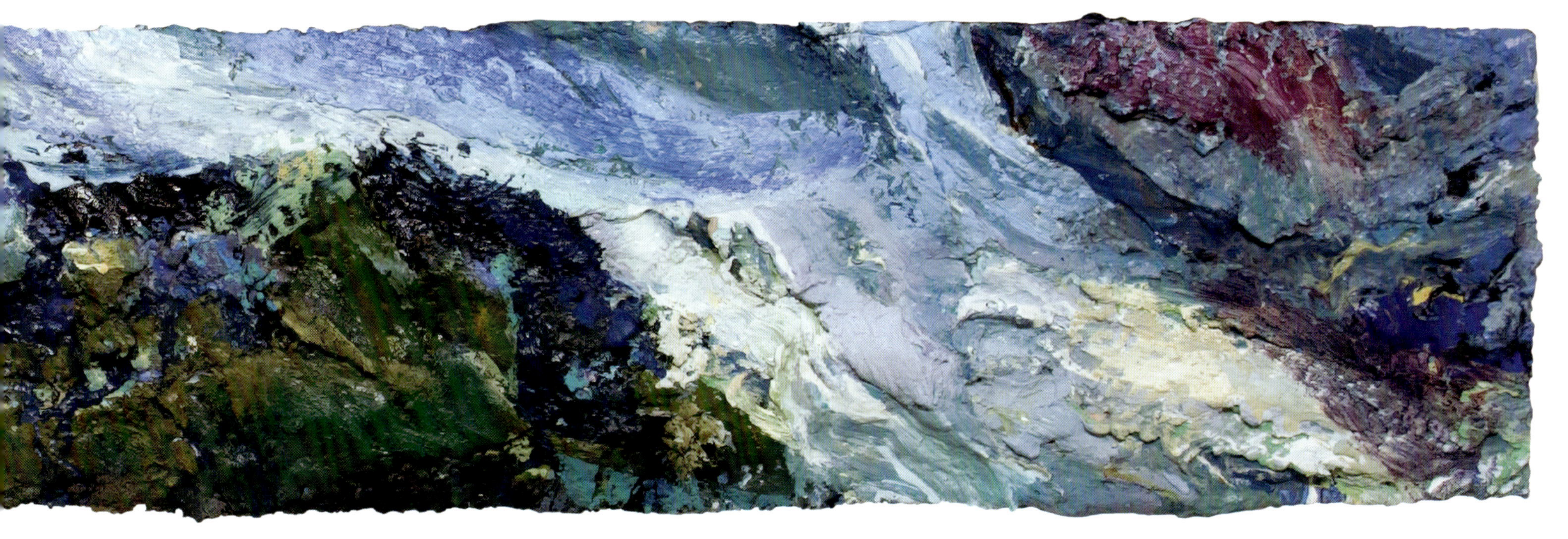

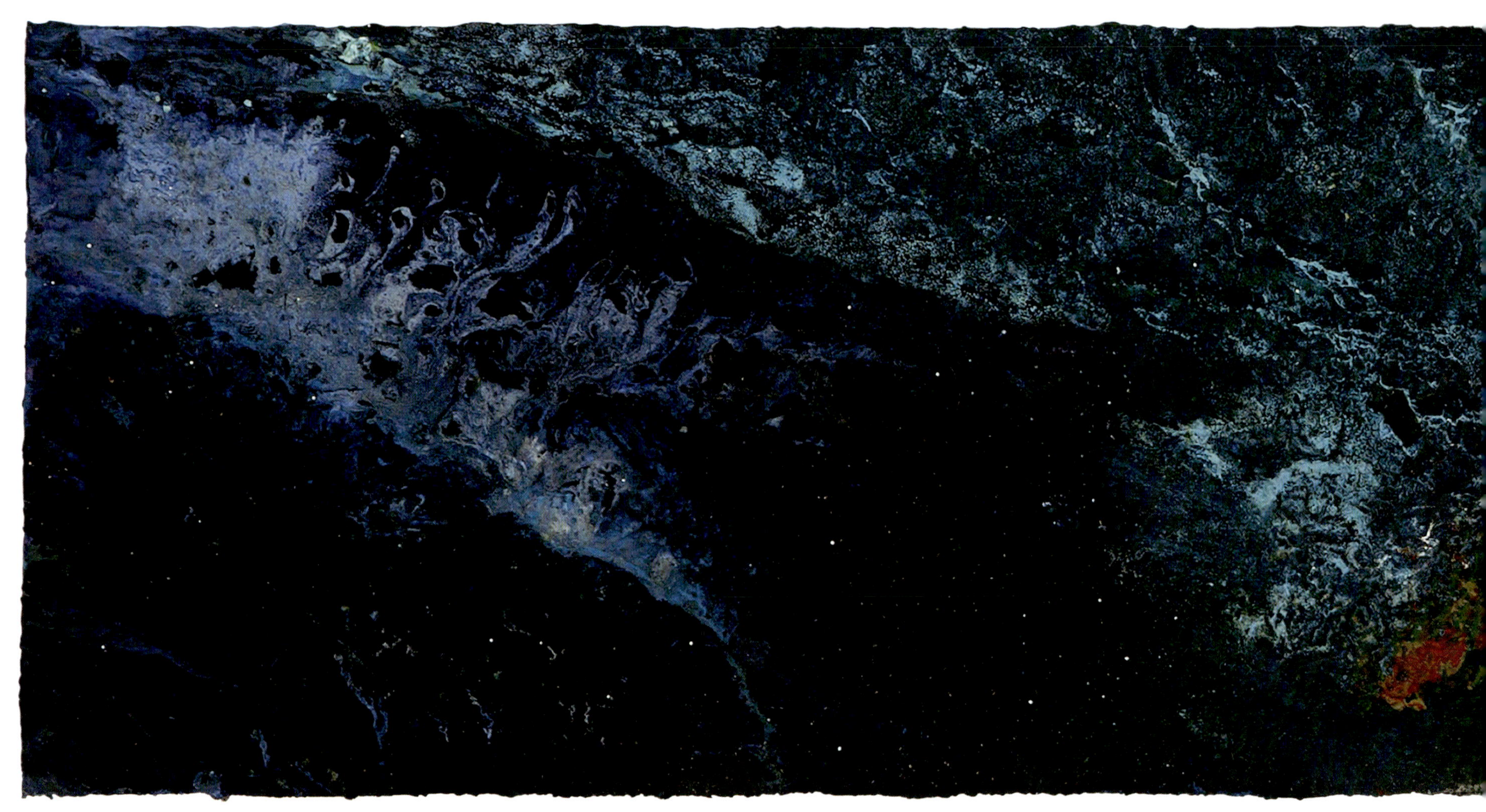

Barfleur, 2007
Oil on panel
12 ½" x 48"
Collection of Anthony J. Moravec,
Columbus, Indiana

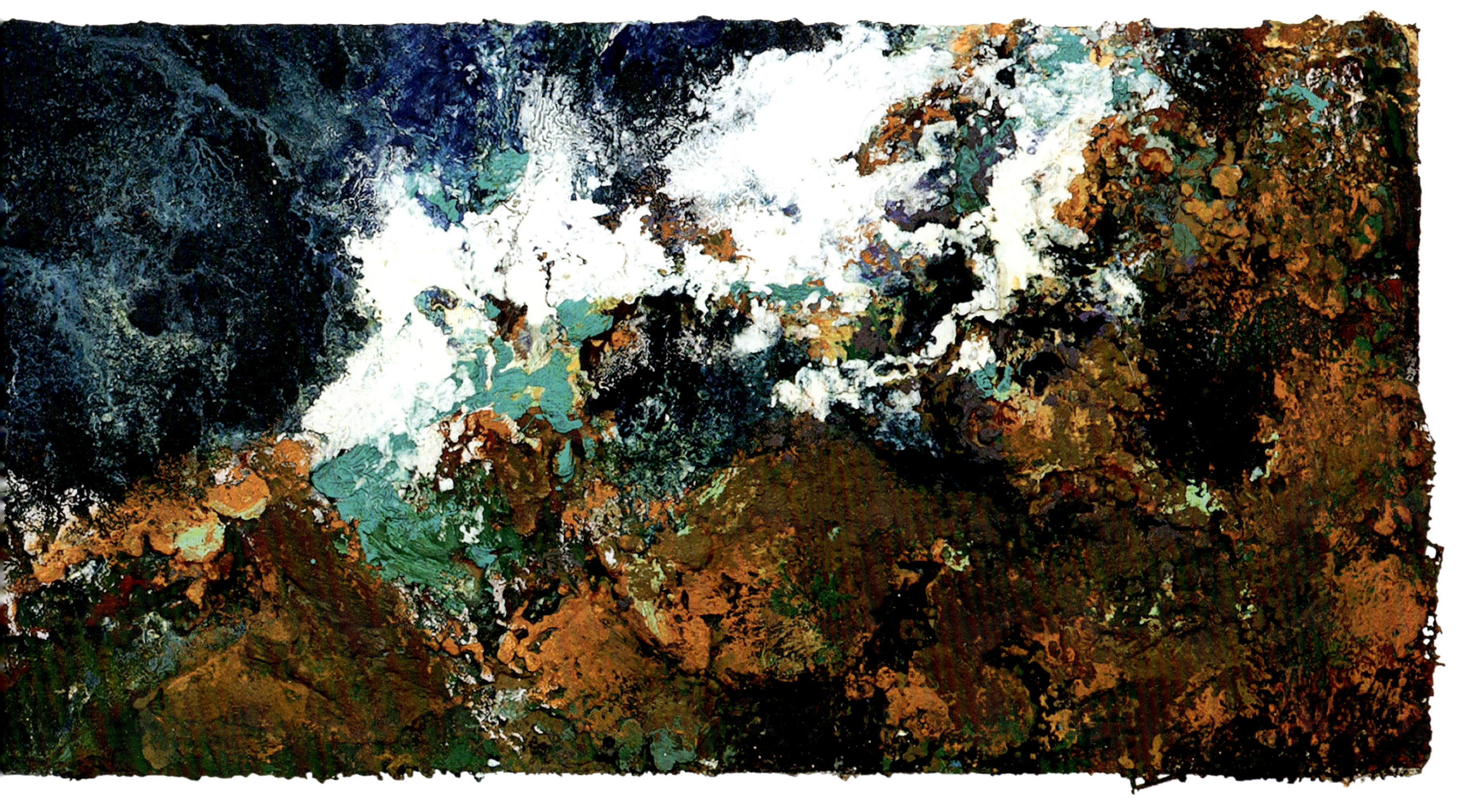

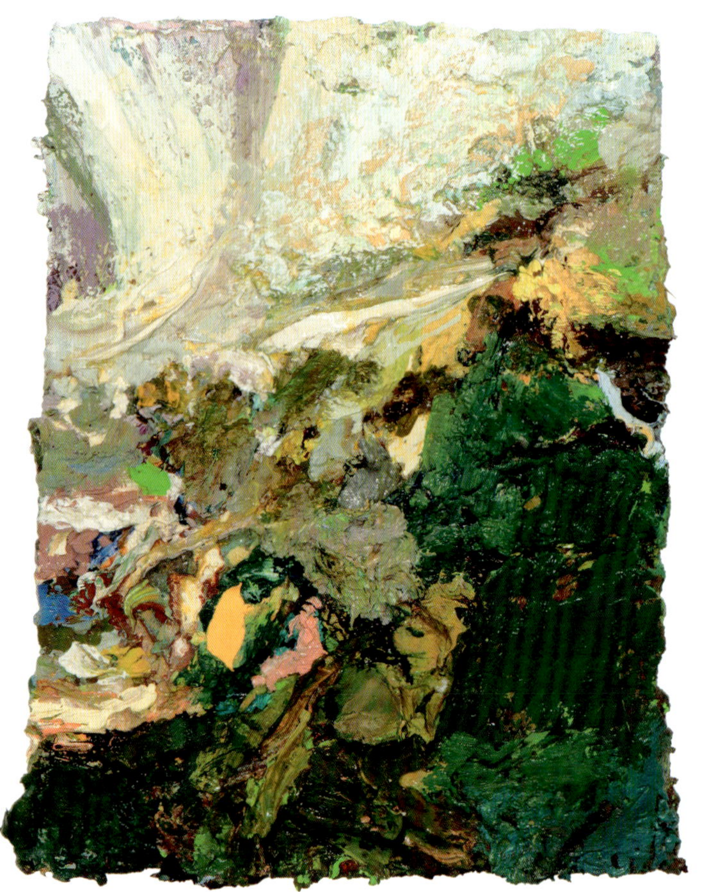

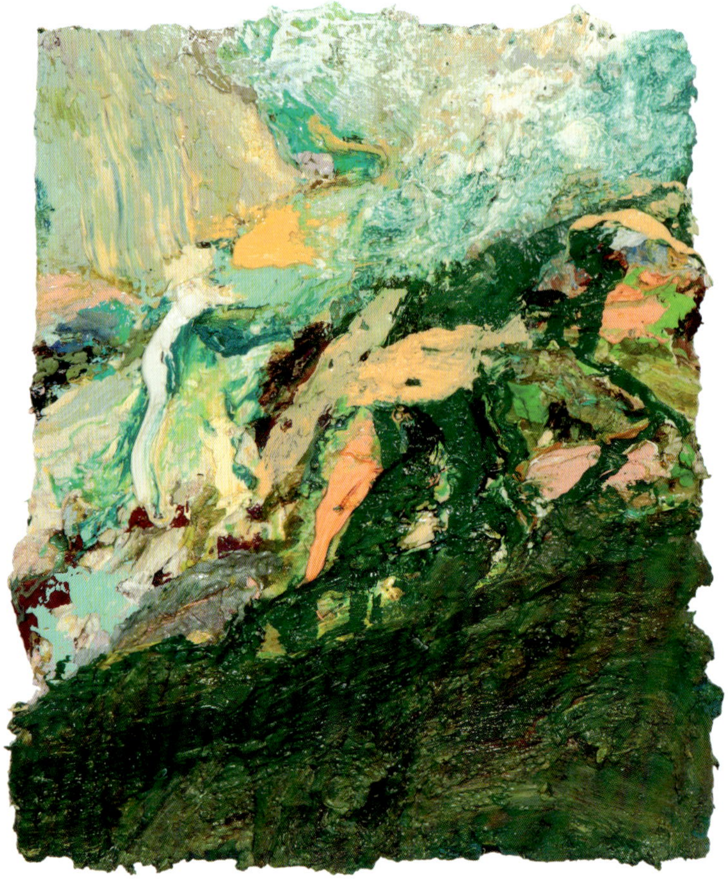

Waterfall II, 2007
Oil on panel
12″ x 9 ¾″
Courtesy, Galerie Beaux-arts
des Amériques, Montréal

Waterfall III, 2007
Oil on panel
12″ x 9 ½″
Courtesy of Galerie Beaux-arts
des Amériques, Montréal

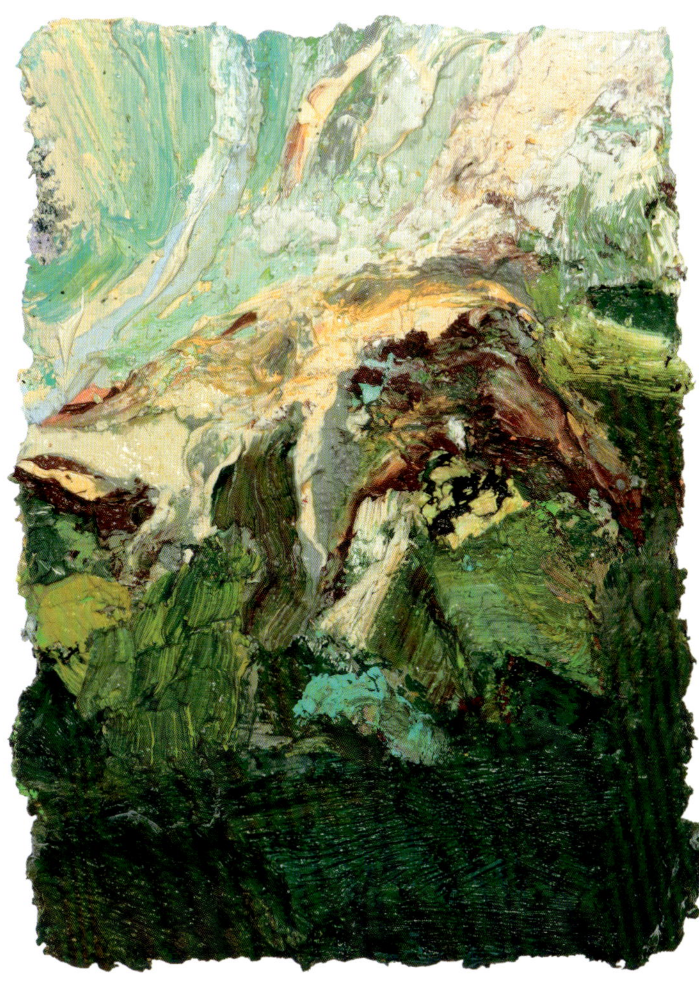

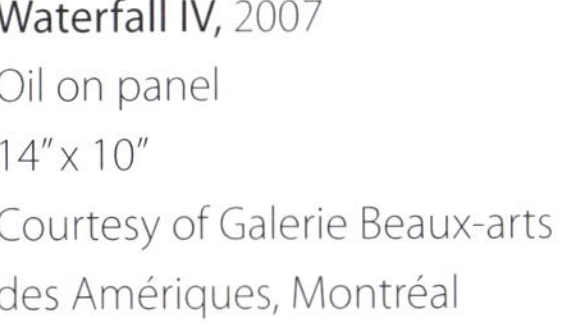

Waterfall IV, 2007
Oil on panel
14″ x 10″
Courtesy of Galerie Beaux-arts
des Amériques, Montréal

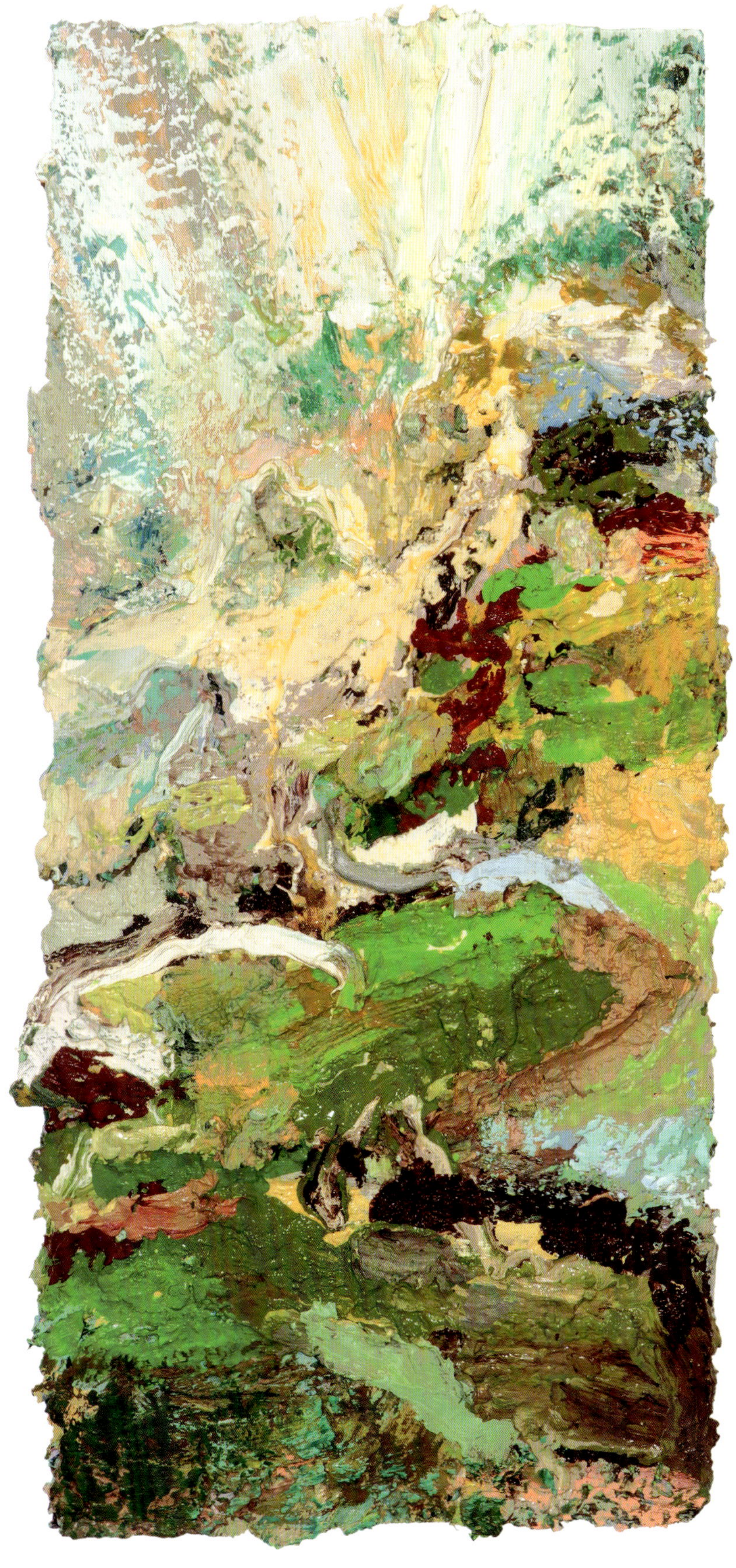

Waterfall V, 2007
Oil on panel
21 ½″ x 10″
Courtesy of Galerie Beaux-arts
des Amériques, Montréal

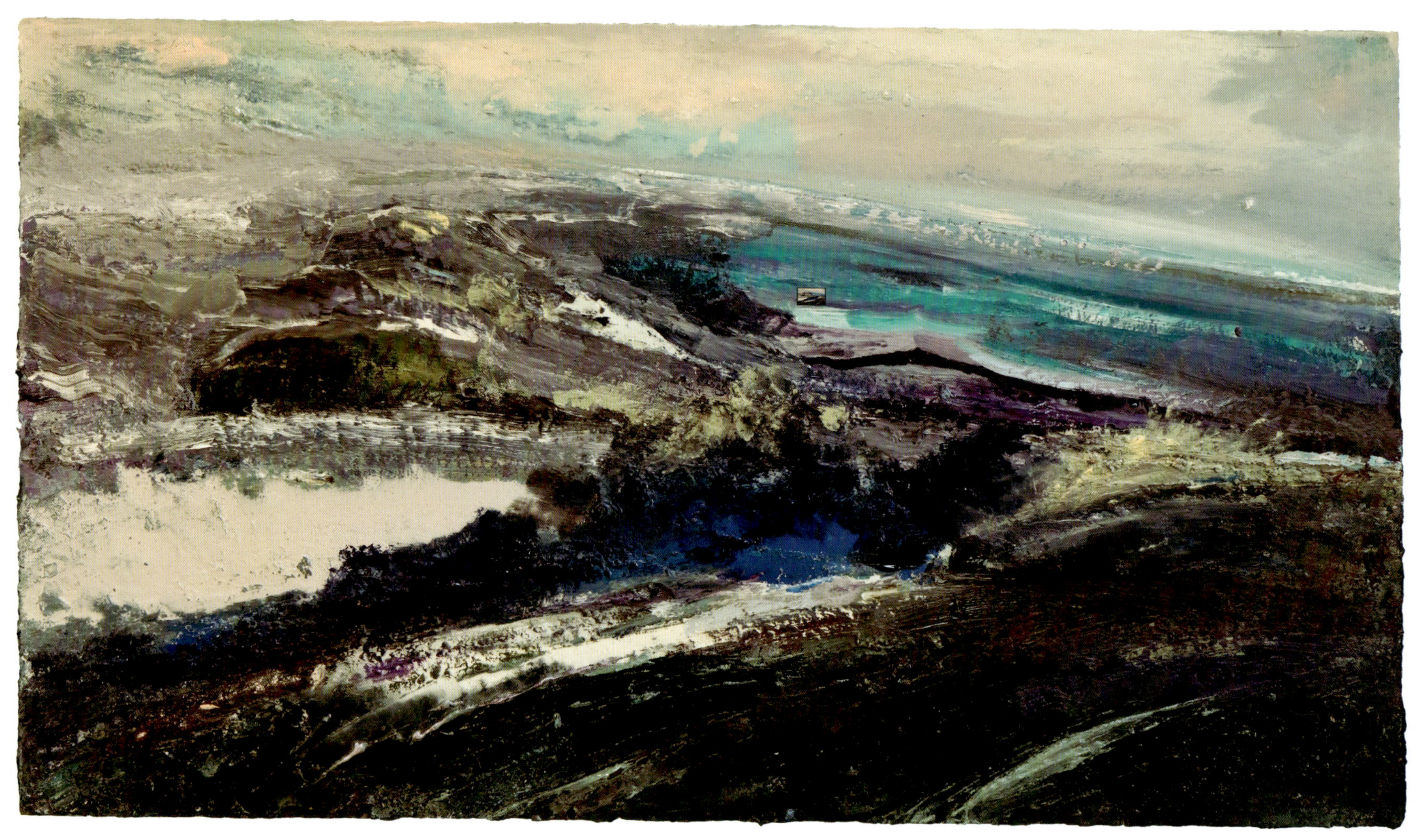

Prince Edward Island, East Point, 2009
Oil on panel
27″ x 49″
Collection of Anthony J. Moravec,
Columbus, Indiana

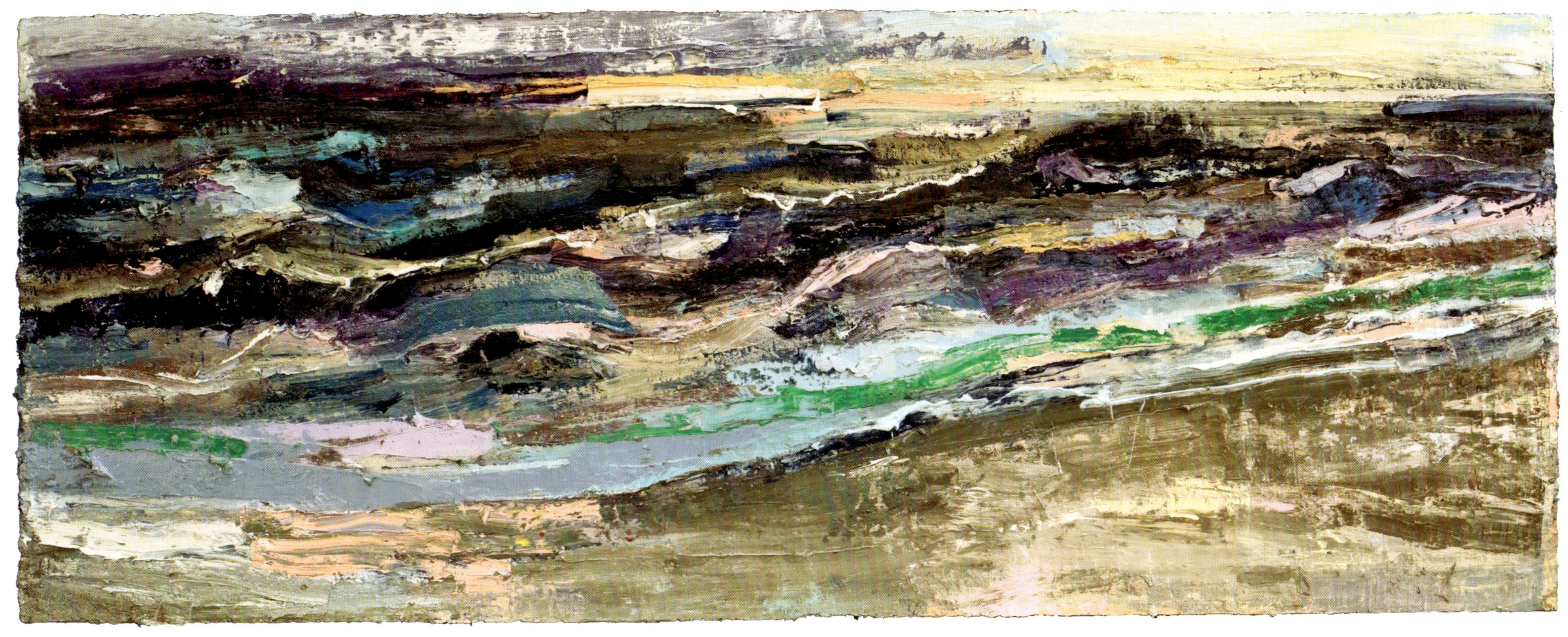

Greenwich Beach, Prince Edward Island, 2009
Oil on panel
30″ x 79 ½″
Collection of Lucie and Larry Glaubinger, New York

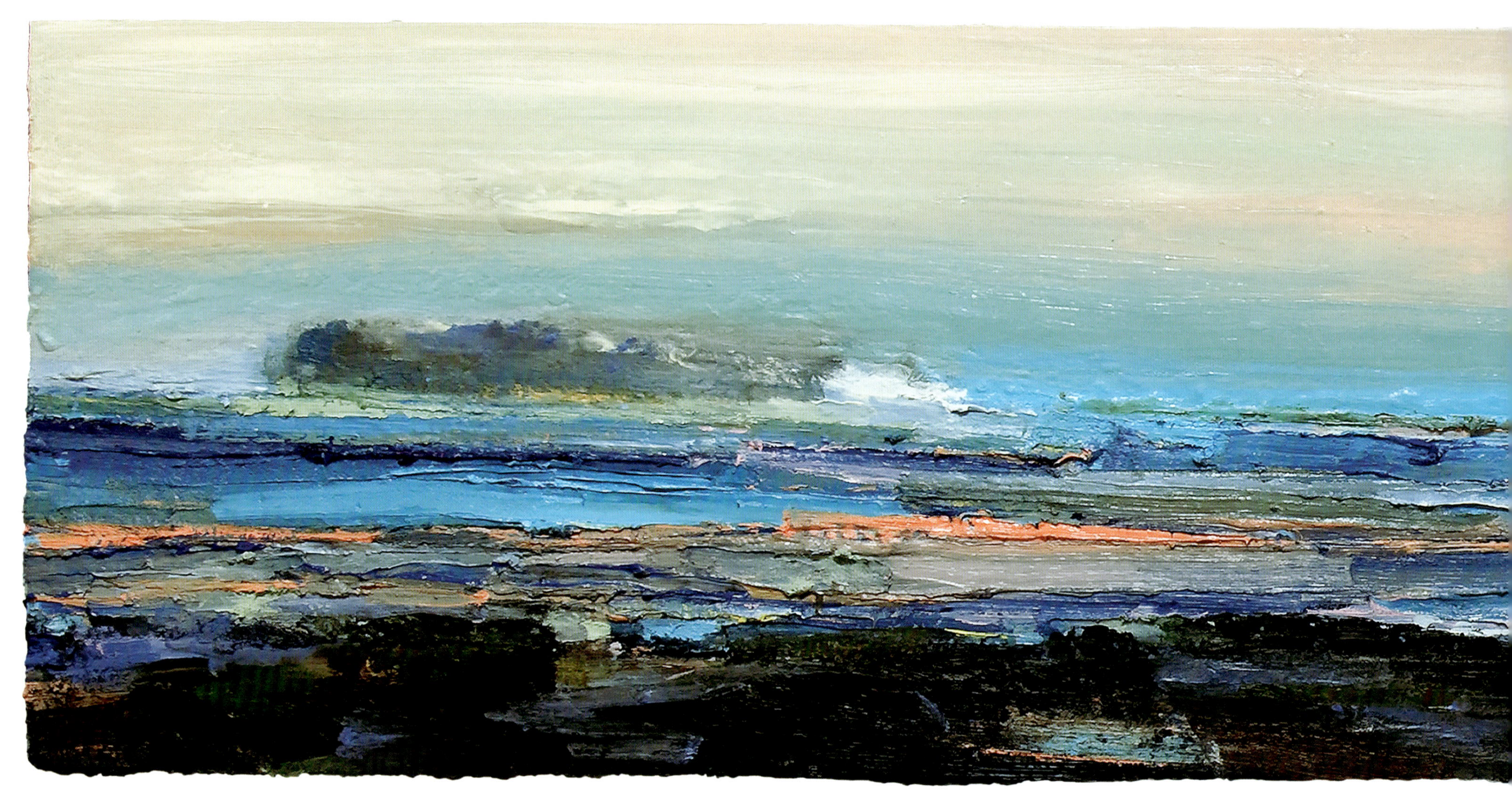

Early September, 5:30 a.m., Oyster Island, Corea, Gulf of Maine, 2009
Oil on panel
22″ x 92″
Collection of Jonlee Andrews and Dan Smith, Bloomington

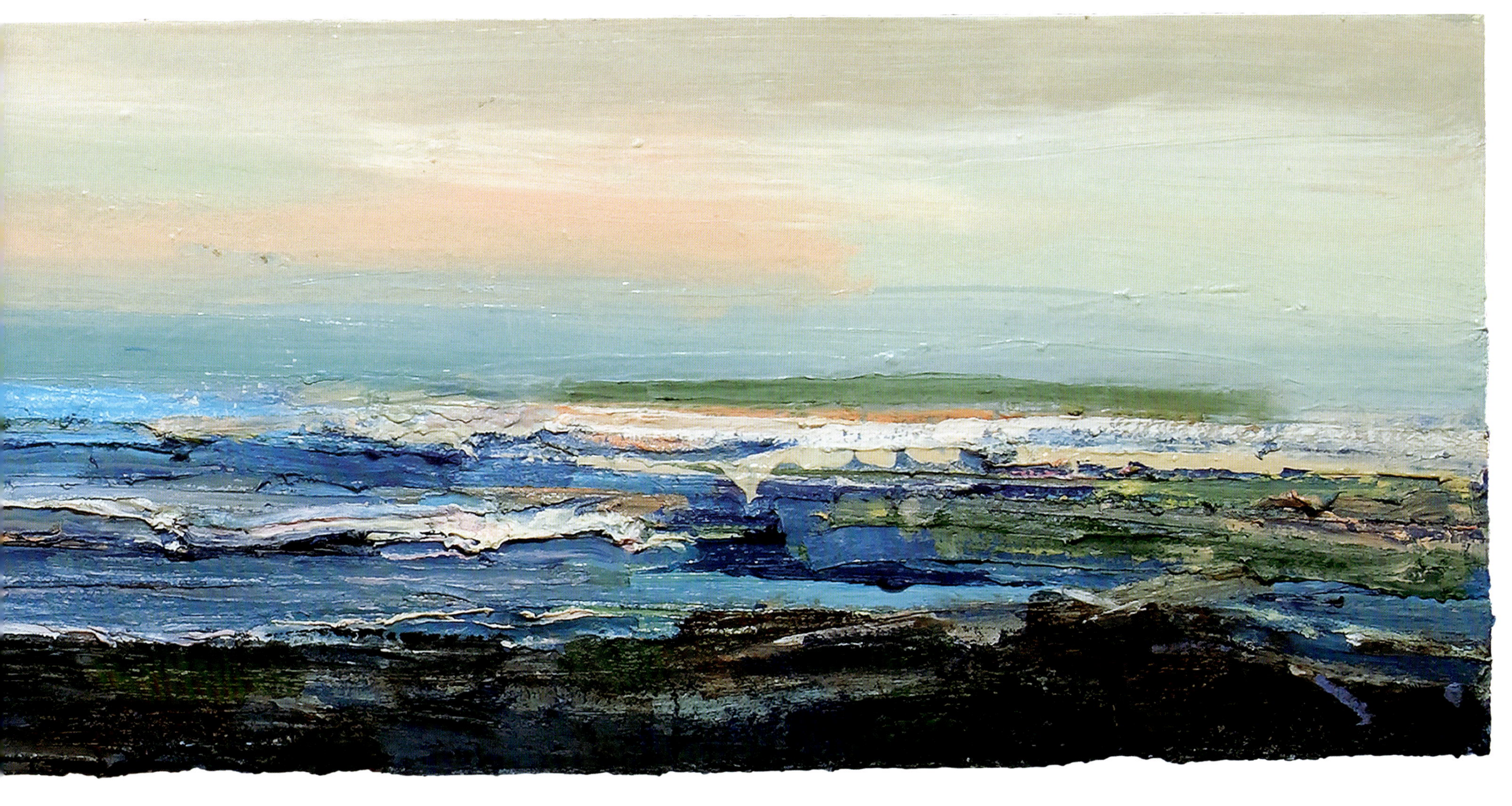

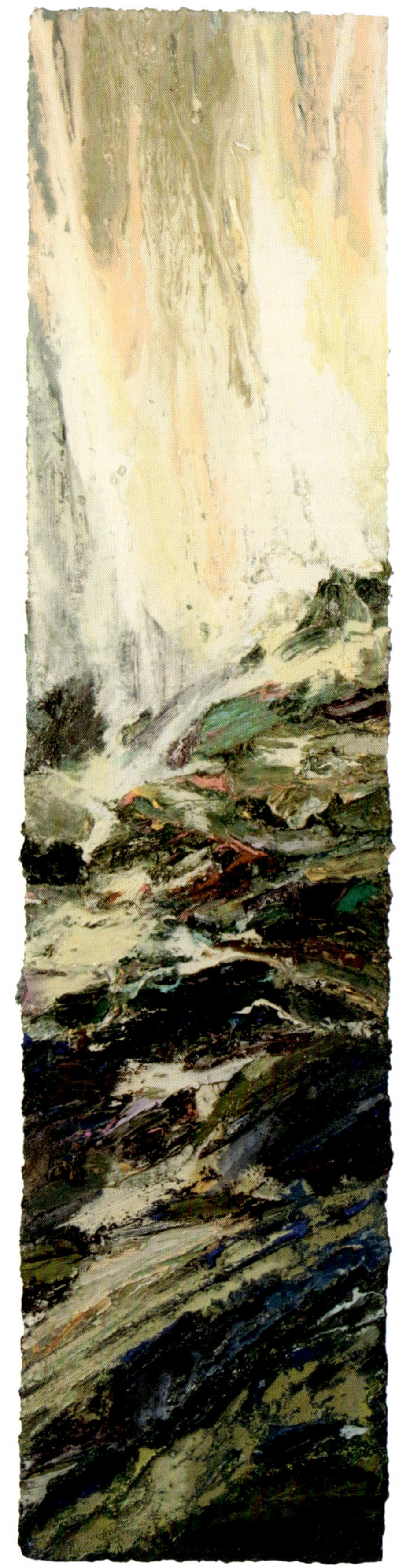

Indiana Waterfall, 2011
Oil on panel
84″ x 20 ½″
Collection of Frank and Frances Kelly,
Zionsville

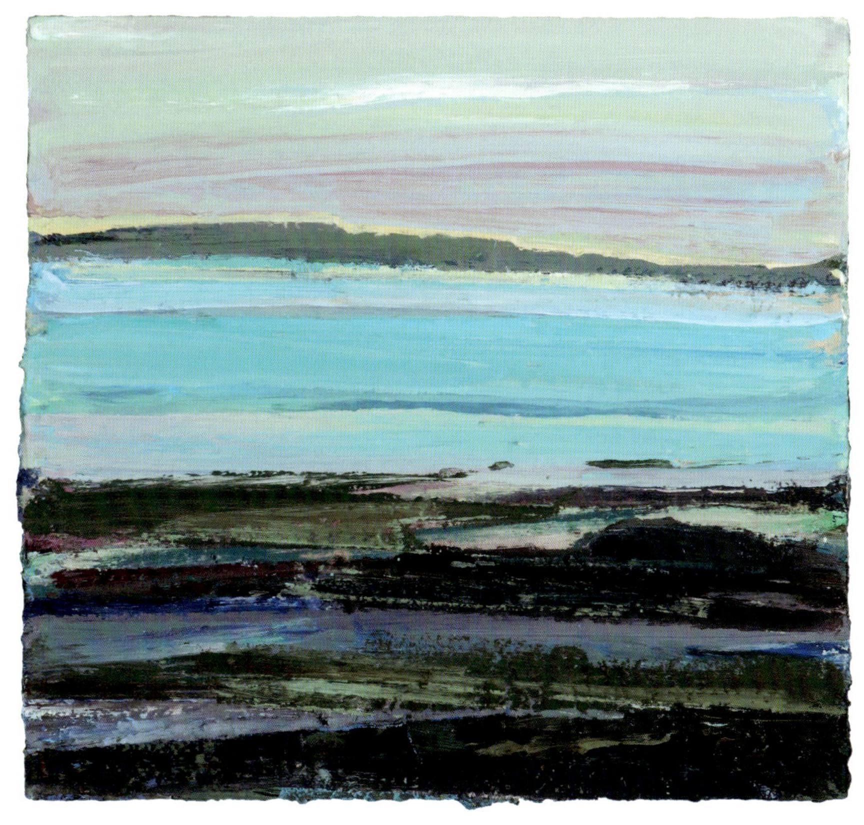

Reflections V, Winter Harbor, Maine, 2011
Oil on panel
18 1/2" x 20"
Collection of Beth and Fred Cate

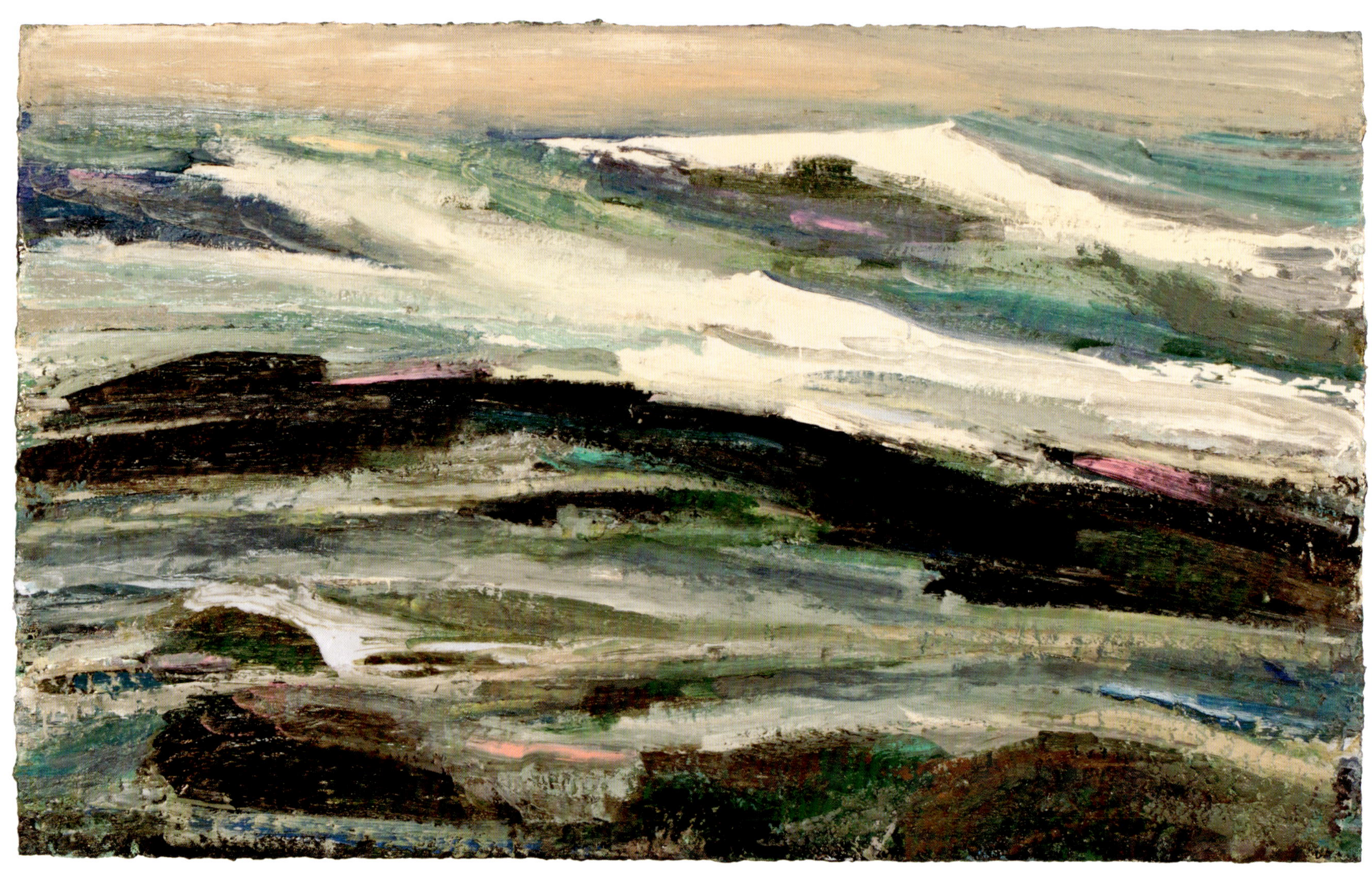

Hurricane Earl, Low Tide, September 2, 10:30 a.m., 2010, Corea, Maine, 2010–11
Oil on panel
36″ x 60″
Private collection, Chicago

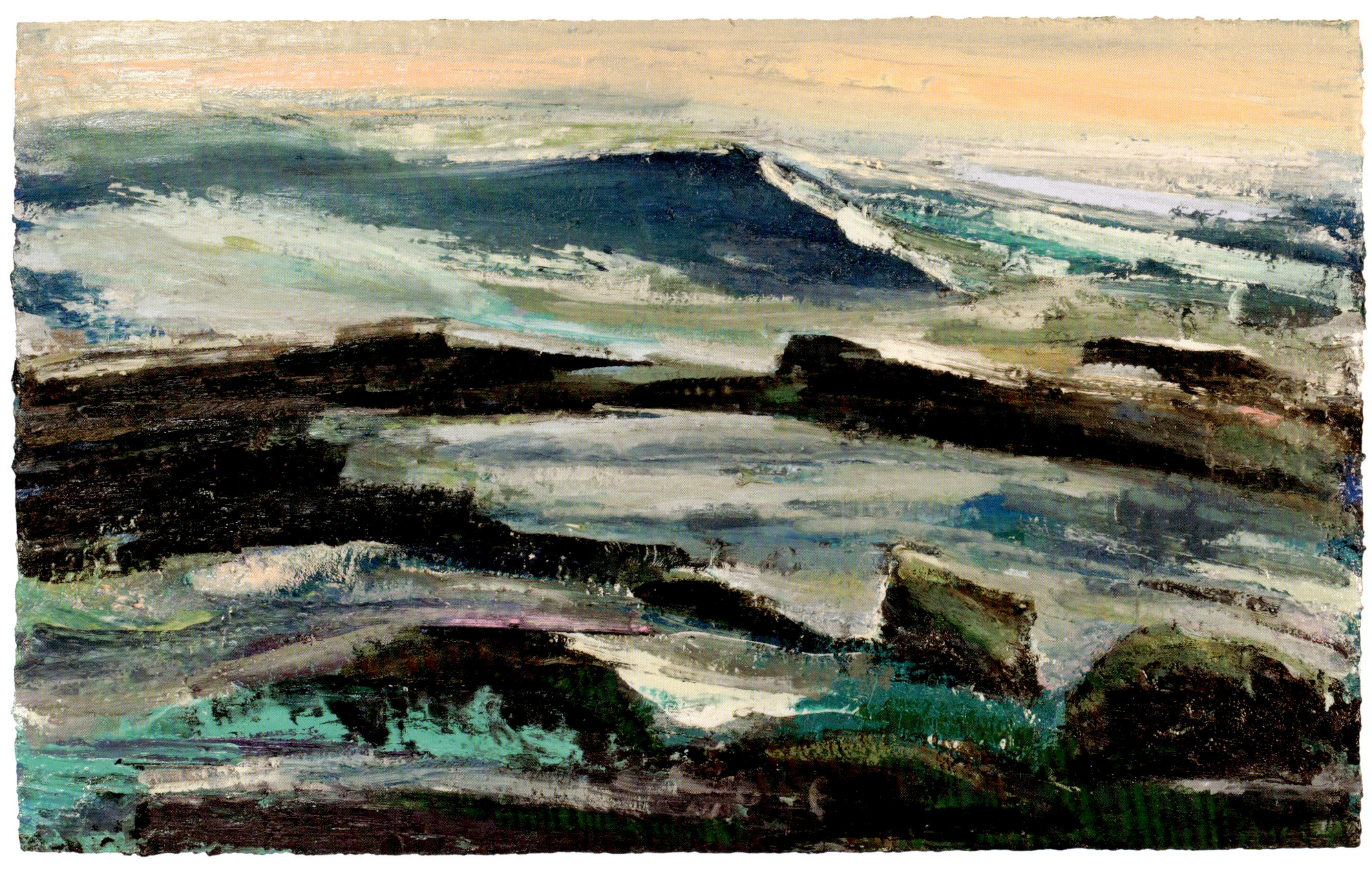

Hurricane Earl, Low Tide, September 2, 11:00 a.m., 2010, Corea, Maine, 2010–11
Oil on panel
36″ x 60″
Private collection, Chicago
[not in exhibition]

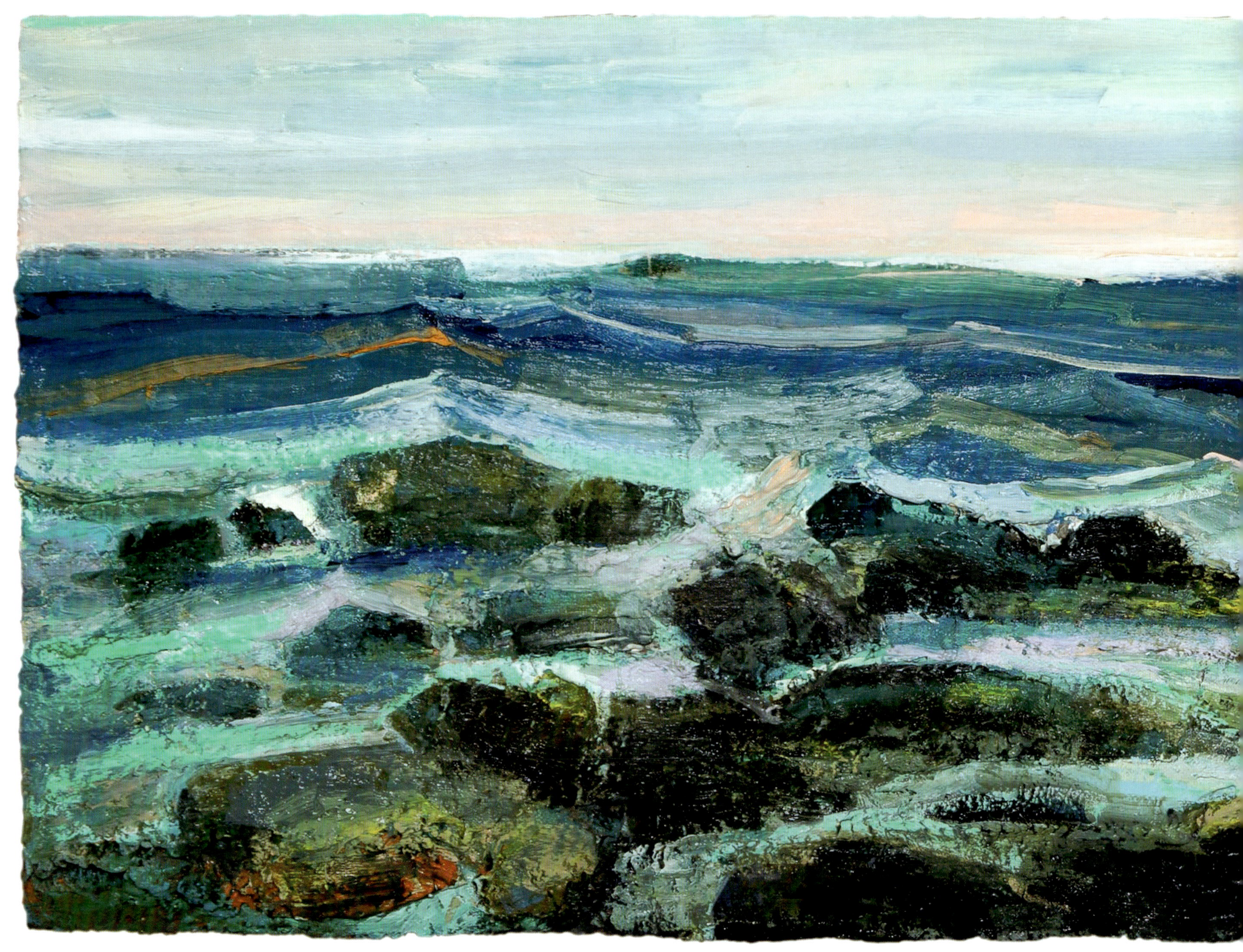

Condon's View of Corea, Maine, 2011
Oil on panel
30" x 83"
Collection of Frank and Frances Kelly,
Zionsville

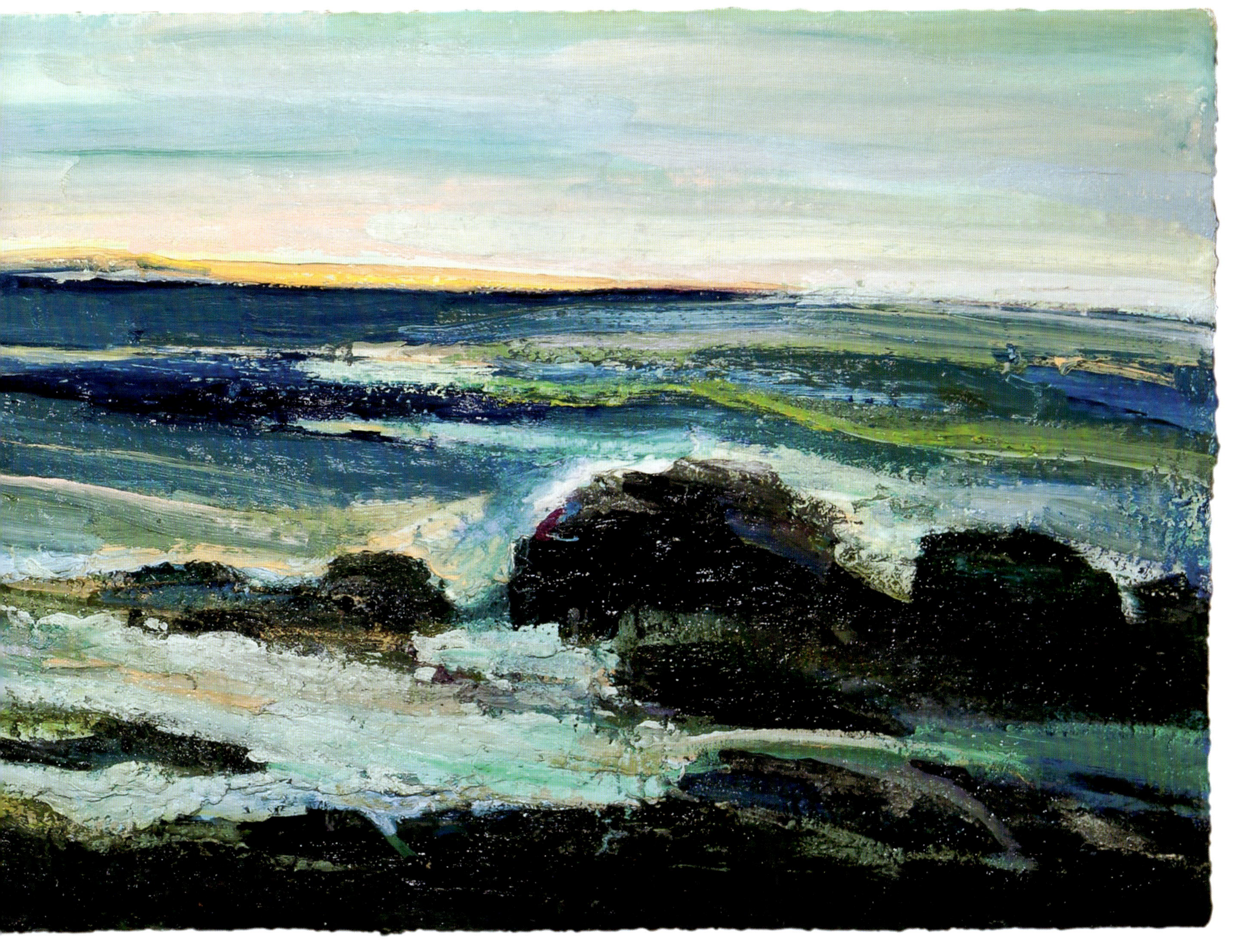

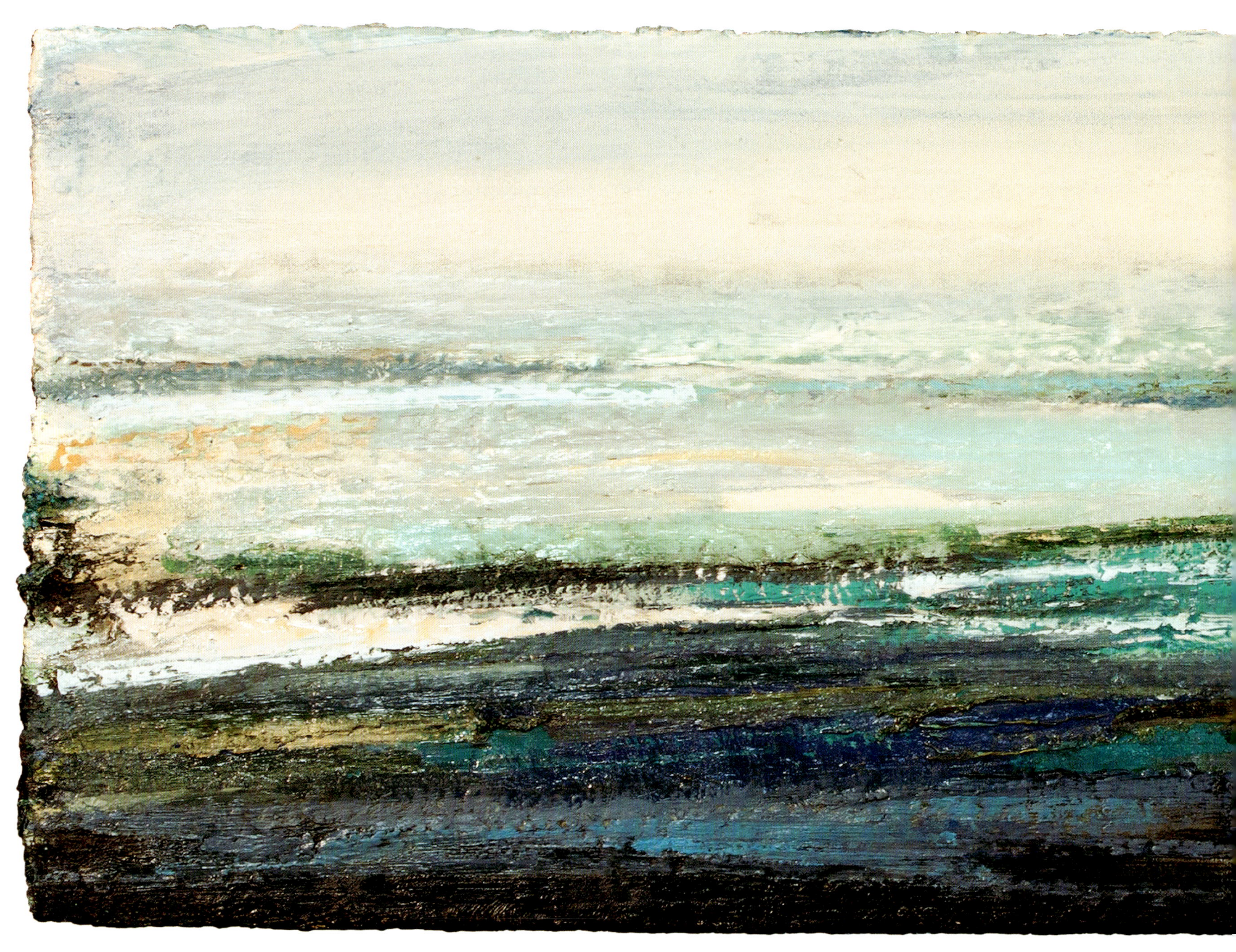

Low Tide, Outer Bar Island,
8:30 a.m., 2010, Corea, Maine, 2010–11
Oil on panel
25 ½″ x 72″
Courtesy of Galerie Beaux-arts des Amériques,
Montréal, Canada

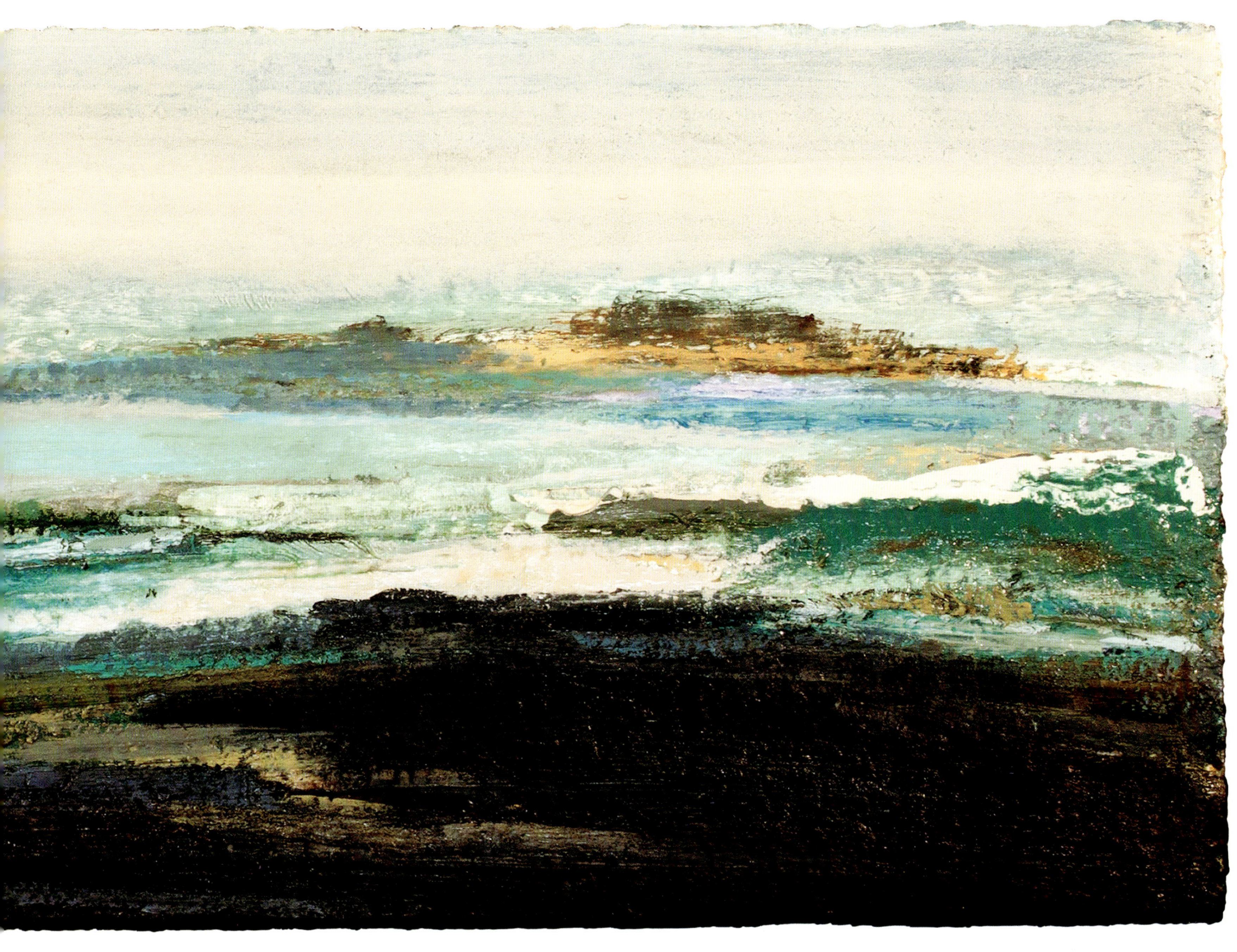

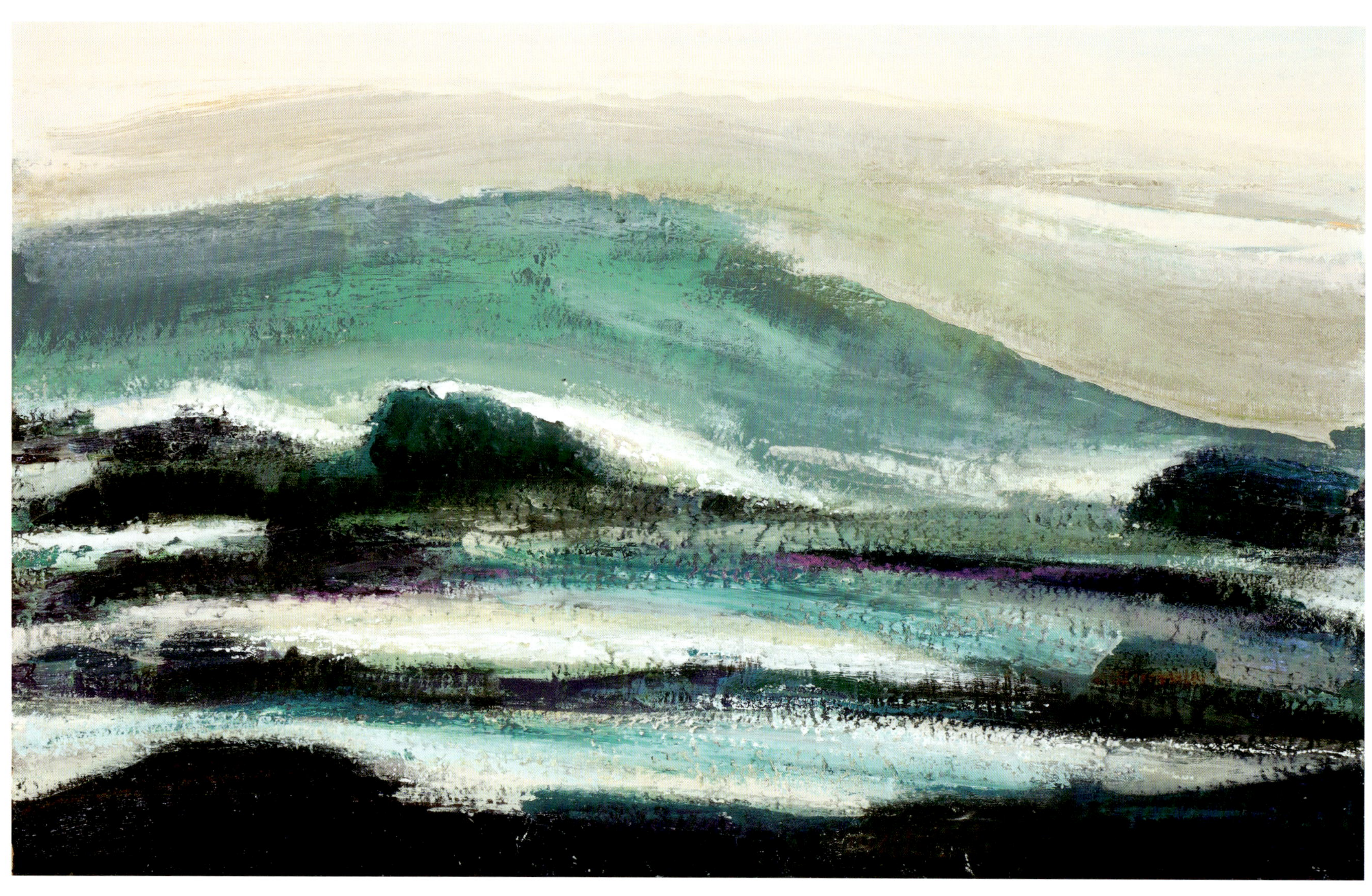

The Wave, 2012
Oil on panel
29 ½″ x 48″
Collection of Heidi and Barry Gealt
[not in exhbition]

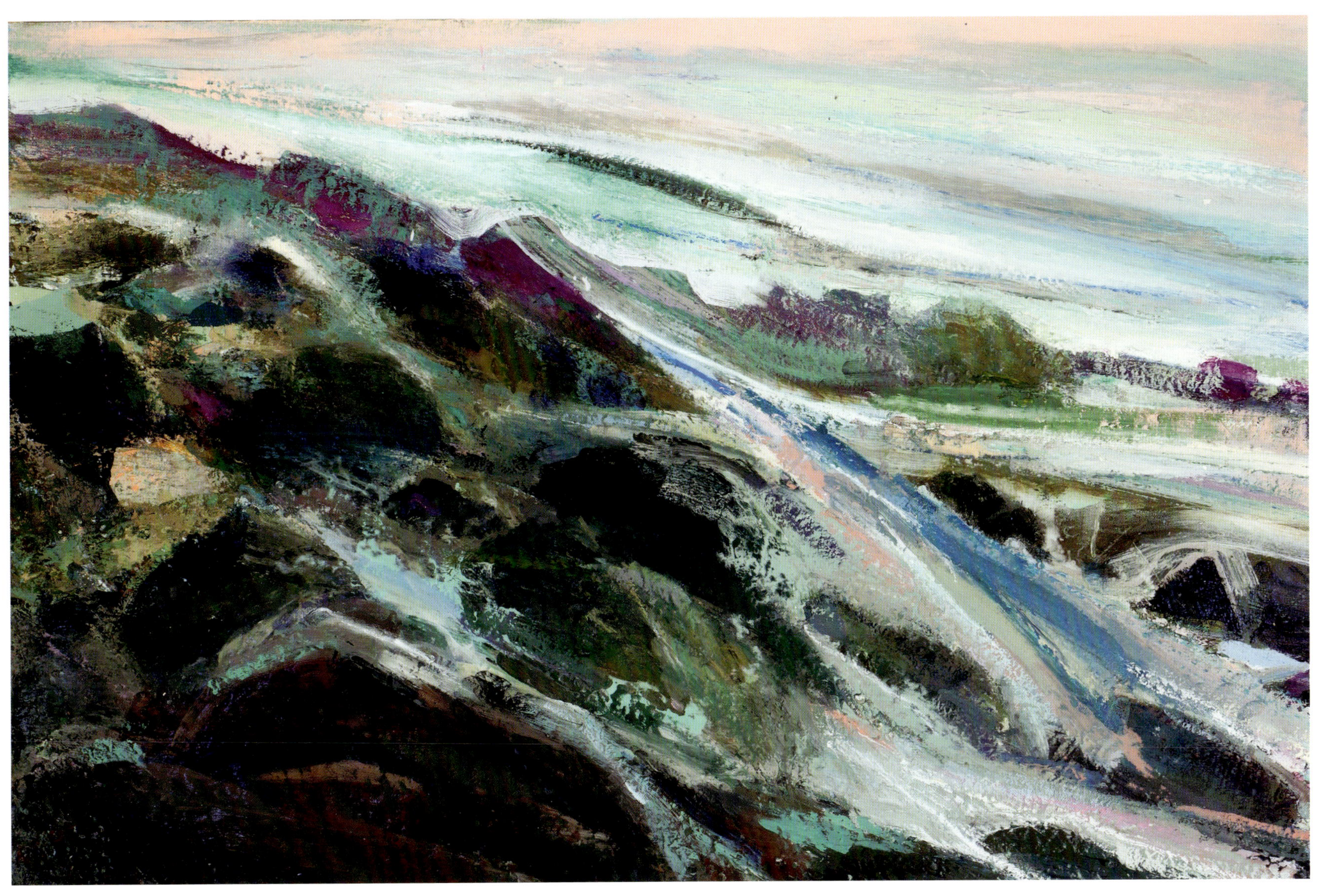

Looking East from Outer Bar Island, Corea, Maine, 2012
Oil on panel
31 ¼″ x 48″
Collection of Heidi and Barry Gealt

Artist's Chronology

Born 1941, Philadelphia, Pennsylvania
Son of Sylvia Benn Gealt and Leonard Gealt
Married Adelheid Medicus in 1969

EDUCATION
1965 MFA, Yale University, graduated with honors (studied with Jack Tworkov, Bernard Chaet, Lester Johnson)
1963 BFA, Philadelphia College of Art (studied with Morris Berd)
1962 Mexico City College, Summer Program

TEACHING and PROGRAM DEVELOPMENT
Professor of Fine Arts, Indiana University, Hope School of Fine Arts, 1969–2007
Director of Studio Program, Indiana University Overseas Program, Florence, Italy, 1984–2007

> Developed undergraduate and graduate studio summer program in Florence, Italy, created assistantships and various other funding sources for students, devised and oversaw the itineraries for students in this program, 1985–2005
> Developed spring break B.F.A. drawing program in Normandy and Giverny, France, March 2004 and March 2007

Visiting Critic, Vermont Studio School, July–August, 1990
Visiting Professor, Queens College, Caumsett Summer Painting Program, Summer 1985
Member, Board of Advisors, Queens College, Caumsett Program, 1985

> Promoted and expanded Indiana University's representation in summer programs including Caumsett, Skowhegan, and the Vermont Studio Center; solicited and developed funding sources for students enrolled in these programs.

Visiting Professor, Kansas City Art Institute, Summer 1973
Founding Chairman, Art Department, Wright State University, 1965–1969

> Developed undergraduate studio and art history program; recruited the faculty

AWARDS
Retired Faculty Grant in Aid of Research, Indiana University, 2012
Retired Faculty Grant in Aid of Research, Indiana University, 2010
Nominated to the National Academy of Design, 2005
College Arts and Humanities Institute Research Grant, Indiana University, Supporting Travel to Normandy, France, 2005
Trustees' Teaching Award, Indiana University, 2004, 2005
Terra Foundation for the Arts, Summer Residency in Giverny, France, 2003
Indiana University Research Grant, 2000
Indiana University Summer Faculty Fellowship, 2000
School of Fine Arts Teaching Excellence Award, Indiana University, 1999, 2000
Senior Faculty Fellowship, Indiana University, 1993
Lilly Endowment Fellowship (Supporting Travel to Japan), 1992–1993
Indiana University Creative Arts Grants, 1981, 1989, 1991, 1992, 1993
Ford Foundation Grant, 1978, 1979
Finalist, Prix-de-Rome, 1971, 1972
Yale University, Alice B. Kimball Travelling Fellowship to Europe, 1965
Yale-Norfolk Summer School, 1964
Provincetown Painting Scholarship, Philadelphia College of Art, 1963
Philadelphia College of Art, Drawing Award, 1962, 1963

EXHIBITIONS
Indiana University Art Museum, Bloomington, *Barry Gealt: Embracing Nature*, Retrospective, October 6 – December 23, 2012
gWatson, Stonington, Maine, *Four Friends*, Group Show, July–August 2012
Galerie Beaux-arts des Amériques, Montréal, Canada Group Show, , January–February 2012
Galerie Beaux-arts des Amériques, Montréal, Canada, Solo Show, April 28–May 22, 2011
Art Naples, Galerie Beaux-arts des Amériques, Naples, Florida, March 2011
Toronto International Art Fair, Galerie Beaux-arts des Amériques, November 2010
Grace Outreach, Metropolitan Club, New York City, Group Show, March 2010
Galerie Beaux-arts des Amériques, Montréal, Canada, Solo Show, May 2009
IU Northwest Gallery for Contemporary Art, Gary, Indiana, *A View from the Passenger's Side Window: Midwest Landscapes*, Group Show, August–September 2008
Mark Ruschman Gallery, Indianapolis, Solo Show, 2008

Collins Lefebvre Stoneberger Gallery, Montréal, Canada, Group Show, March 2007
Hope School of Fine Arts Gallery, Indiana University, Bloomington, Faculty Show, Spring 2007
Hope School of Fine Arts Gallery, Indiana University, Bloomington, Solo Show, February 2006
Hope School of Fine Arts Gallery, Indiana University, Bloomington, Faculty Show, Spring 2005
Kunsthandlung Osper, Cologne, Germany, *Four Major Works*, Spring 2005
Mark Ruschman Gallery, Indianapolis, Group Show, September 2004
DePauw University, Greencastle, Indiana, *Terra Firma: Five Contemporary Indiana Artists Paint the Landscape,* August–October 2003
Kunsthanlung Osper, Cologne, Germany, Group Show, Summer 2003
Mark Ruschman Gallery, Indianapolis, Solo Show, April 2003
Las Vegas Art Museum, *Private Eye…Public View: Goodman–Duffy Collection of Contemporary Art*, November– December 2002
Kunsthandlung Osper, Cologne, Germany, Solo Show, October–November 2001
Mark Ruschman Gallery, Indianapolis, Solo Show, March 2000
Midwest Museum of American Art, Elkhart, Indiana, *The Nature of Landscape: Hoosier Landscapes Past and Present* September–October 1998
Synchronicity Space, New York City, Two-Person Show, September 1997
Synchronicity Space, New York City, Group Show, January 1997
Indiana University Art Museum, Bloomington, *One Hundred Year Anniversary*, Faculty Show, January 1996
Fontbonne Gallery, Fontbonne College, St. Louis, *The Nature of Landscape*, Group Show, October 1995
Snite Museum of Art, Notre Dame University, South Bend, Indiana, Solo Show, June–September 1995
Indiana University Art Museum, Bloomington, *Intersections*, System-wide Faculty Show, February 1995
Valparaiso University Museum of Art, Valparaiso, Indiana, Solo Show, January 1995
Mark Ruschman Gallery, Indianapolis, Solo Show, September 1994
Indiana University Department of Fine Arts Gallery, Bloomington, Faculty Show, Bloomington, 1993
Bradley Drawing and Print Invitational, March–April 1993
Mark Ruschman Gallery, Indianapolis,Three-Person Landscape Show, April 1991
University of Dayton, Dayton, Ohio, *Recent Paintings and a Decade of Drawings*, March 1991
Indiana University Department of Fine Arts Gallery, Bloomington, Faculty Show, Bloomington, 1991
Twentieth-Century Gallery, Williamsburg, Virginia, Solo Show, October 1990
University of Dayton, Dayton, Ohio, Works-on-Paper Show, March 1990
Bowery Gallery, New York City, Solo Show, May–June 1989
Curator's Choice, Munster, Indiana, May–June, 1989
Indiana University Department of Fine Arts Gallery, Bloomington, Faculty Show, 1989
Gross-McCleaf Gallery, Philadelphia, Group Figurative Exhibition, March 1987
Bank Street School Gallery, New York City, Group Landscape Exhibition, Fall 1986
Indiana University Department of Fine Arts Gallery, Bloomington, Faculty Show, 1986
Thiel College, Greenville, Pennsylvania, Solo Show, January–February 1985
DePauw University Art Gallery, Greencastle, Indiana, Solo Show, September 1984
Westminster College, New Castle, Pennsylvania, Solo Show, November–December, 1984
Indiana University Department of Fine Arts Gallery, Bloomington, Faculty Show, 1984
Joanna Dean Gallery, New York City, Group Show, January–February, 1983
Evansville Museum of Arts and Science, *Prints from Echo Press*, Group Show, September–October 1982
Sheldon Swope Art Gallery, Terre Haute, Indiana, *Prints from Echo Press*, Group Show, October–November 1982
Zaks Gallery, Chicago, Drawing Show, September 1982
Charlotte Kemper Gallery, Kansas City Art Institute, Kansas City, Missouri, Invitational Drawing Show, Fall 1982
Dorry Gates Gallery, Kansas City, Missouri, Group Show, Spring1981
Sheldon Memorial Art Gallery, University of Nebraska, Lincoln, Solo Show, Fall 1981
Indianapolis Art League, Group Show, Indianapolis, Fall 1980
Indiana University Art Museum, Bloomington, Solo Drawing Show, Summer 1979
Franklin College, Franklin, Indiana, Solo Show, 1979
Sheldon Swope Art Gallery, Terre Haute, Indiana, Group Show, Fall 1979
DePauw University, Greencastle, Indiana, Drawing Show, Invitational, Fall 1978
Hobart College, Geneva, New York, Solo Show, 1977
North Carolina University, Cullowhee, North Carolina, Painting Invitational, Fall 1976
Kansas City Art Institute, Kansas City, Missouri, Two-Person Show with Donald Perlis, 1975
University of Wisconsin, Green Bay, *Representational Figure Painting in America*, Fall 1973
Bard College, Annandale-on-Hudson, New York, Solo Show, Fall 1973
Hollins College, Hollins, Virginia, Solo Show, Fall 1972

LECTURES
University of New Hampshire, Durham, December 2007
University of Memphis, Memphis, Tennessee, October 2007
Indiana University, Henry Radford School of Fine Arts, February 2006
Pennsylvania Academy of Fine Arts, Philadelphia, December 2005
University of South Carolina, Columbia, April 2005
University of Washington, Seattle, October 2004
Indiana University, College of Arts and the Humanities, March 2004
Terra Foundation for the Arts, Giverny, France, July 2003
University of New Hampshire, Durham, November 2000
Indianapolis Museum of Art, "Fernand Leger," October 1999
Indianapolis Museum of Art, "Hans Hoffman," November 1998
Southwest Missouri State University, West Plains, September 1998
Elkhart, Indiana, "The Nature of Landscape," September 1998
University of Missouri, Columbia, October 1997
University of Illinois, Edwardsville, April 1997
De Pauw University, Greencastle, Indiana, December 1996
University of Louisville, Louisville, Kentucky, April 1996
Fontbonne College, St. Louis, Missouri, November 1995
Notre Dame University, Snite Museum of Art, "American Landscape Painting," September 1995
Valparaiso University Museum of Art, Valparaiso, Indiana,

"The Hidden Nature of Indiana," January 1995
Indiana University Art Museum, "To Take a Journey," Bloomington, 1994
Friends of Art, Herron School of Art, "To Take a Journey," Indianapolis, 1994
American University, Washington, D.C., March, 1993
Washington University, St. Louis, Missouri, January 1992
University of Dayton, Dayton, Ohio, March 1991
Southeastern Louisiana University, Hammond, March 1991
Bowdoin College, Bowdoin, Maine, November 1990
University of New Hampshire, Durham, November 1990
Colby College, Waterville, Maine, November 1990
Vermont Studio School, Johnson, July 1990
Dartmouth College, Hanover, New Hampshire, July 1990
Drury College, Springfield, Missouri, April 1990
Southwest Missouri State University, Springfield, April 1990
University of Dayton, Dayton, Ohio, March 1990
Queens College, Caumsett Summer Program, July 1988
Dartmouth College, Hanover, New Hampshire, April 1987
Kansas City Art Institute, Kansas City, Missouri, Spring 1985 (with Donald Perlis)
Thiel College, Greenville, Pennsylvania, November 1984
Westminster College, New Castle, Pennsylvania, November 1984
Wright State University, Dayton, Ohio, October 1984
DePauw University, Greencastle, Indiana, September 1984
Ohio University, Athens, "On Being an Artist," April 1984
Sheldon Memorial Art Gallery, Lincoln, Nebraska, Fall 1981
Hobart College, Geneva, New York, "On Artists' Debts to Other Artists," Fall 1977

PUBLISHED IN

Research and Creative Activity, Visual Arts, Indiana University, Spring 2005
Osper Gallery, *Barry Gealt*, brochure with an essay by Wally Goodman, Cologne, Germany, Spring 2005
Nuvo, Visual Arts Review, "Textural Fetish," Indianapolis, May 2003
Osper Gallery, *Amerikanische Landschaften*, brochure with an essay by Reiner Budde, Cologne, Germany, 2001
Roger Winter, *On Drawing*, Collegiate Press, San Diego, 1991

SELECTED PUBLIC and PRIVATE COLLECTIONS:

Sue and Curt Anderson, Las Vegas
Jonlee Andrews and Daniel Smith, Bloomington, Indiana
Alfred Bader, Milwaukee
Christine Baeumler, St. Paul, Minnesota
Faegre Baker Daniels, LLP, Indianapolis
Gabriele and Dieter Bamberger, Cologne, Germany
Sho Banno, Osaka, Japan
Rigel Barber, Chicago
Nancy and Robert Barnes, Searsport, Maine
Francesco Battazzi, Florence, Italy
Antonetta and Giuseppe Bergamini, Udine, Italy
Elisa dal Canto, Milan, Italy
Beth and Fred Cate, Bloomington, Indiana
Mrs. Chisato, Kyoto, Japan
Amanda and Andrea Ciccarelli, Bloomington, Indiana
Dayton Art Institute, Dayton, Ohio
Beth Edwards, Dayton, Ohio
Telene and William Eddington, Indianapolis, Indiana
Dorothy Frapwell, Bloomington, Indiana
Margareta San di Giacomo, Udine, Italy
Maureen and William Friel, Bloomington, Indiana
Clara and Piero Funis, Florence, Italy
Lucille and Larry Glaubinger, New York City
Patrick Duffy and Wally Goodman, Las Vegas
Midge and Robert Greising, Indianapolis
Hallmark Corporation Art Collection, Kansas City, Missouri
Ann and Rusty Harrison, Attica, Indiana
John Haskin, Haskin, Lauter and LaRue, Indianapolis
Diemut and Walter Heller, San Diego
Christine and Nick Hill, Columbus, Ohio
Indiana University Art Museum, Bloomington
Indiana State Museum, Indianapolis
Mr. and Mrs. Jamaguchi, Osaka, Japan
Debbie Kahn, Washington, D.C.
Frank and Francis Kelly, Zionsville, Indiana
Pat and Robert Kingsley, Bloomington, Indiana
Marian Knauf, Berlin, Germany
Thies Knauf, Shellbyville, Indiana, and Lilienhof, Germany
Charles Lanham, Indianapolis
Lisa McKee Lanham and Michael W. Halstead, Indianapolis
Mr. and Mrs. Chuck Loving, South Bend, Indiana
Sunshine Luciano, New York City
Robert Mann, Bloomington, Indiana
Katherine May, Hudson, New Hampshire
Michael McRobbie, Indiana University
Katherine and Gustav Medicus, Kent, Ohio
Gloria and Ulrich Middeldorf collection, Florence, Italy
Joseph Miller, Indianapolis
Anthony J. Moravec, Columbus, Indiana
Jennifer Moses, Boston
Nicki Noyes, Bloomington, Indiana
Dorit and Gerald Paul, Indianapolis
Pamela Parsons, Scranton, Pennsylvania
Mark Ruschman, Indianapolis
Carol and Dean Porter, South Bend, Indiana
Vildan and Muhittin Serin, Istanbul, Turkey
Lois and Terre Schott, Fort Lauderdale, Florida
Snite Museum of Art, Notre Dame University, South Bend, Indiana
Kerry Dinneen and Sam Sutphin, Indianapolis
Toyota, Cologne, Germany
Trisolini Gallery, The Ohio University College of Fine Arts, Athens
Udine Museum of Modern Art, Udine, Italy
Celicia and Henry Upper, Bloomington, Indiana
Valparaiso Museum of Art, Valparaiso University, Valparaiso, Indiana
Las Vegas Art Museum
Ed Voris, Bedford, Indiana
Wabash College, Crawfordsville, Indiana
Jenna Walls, Indianapolis
Mr. Watanabe, Kyoto, Japan
Jeanette and Roger Winter, Frankfort, Maine
Christina and Sandro Zecchi, Florence, Italy
Rosella and Massimo Zecchi, Florence, Italy

GALLERY REPRESENTATION

Ruschman Fine Art, Indianapolis
Galerie Beaux-arts des Amériques, Montréal, Canada
Kunsthandlung Osper, Cologne, Germany
gWatson Gallery, Stonington, Maine

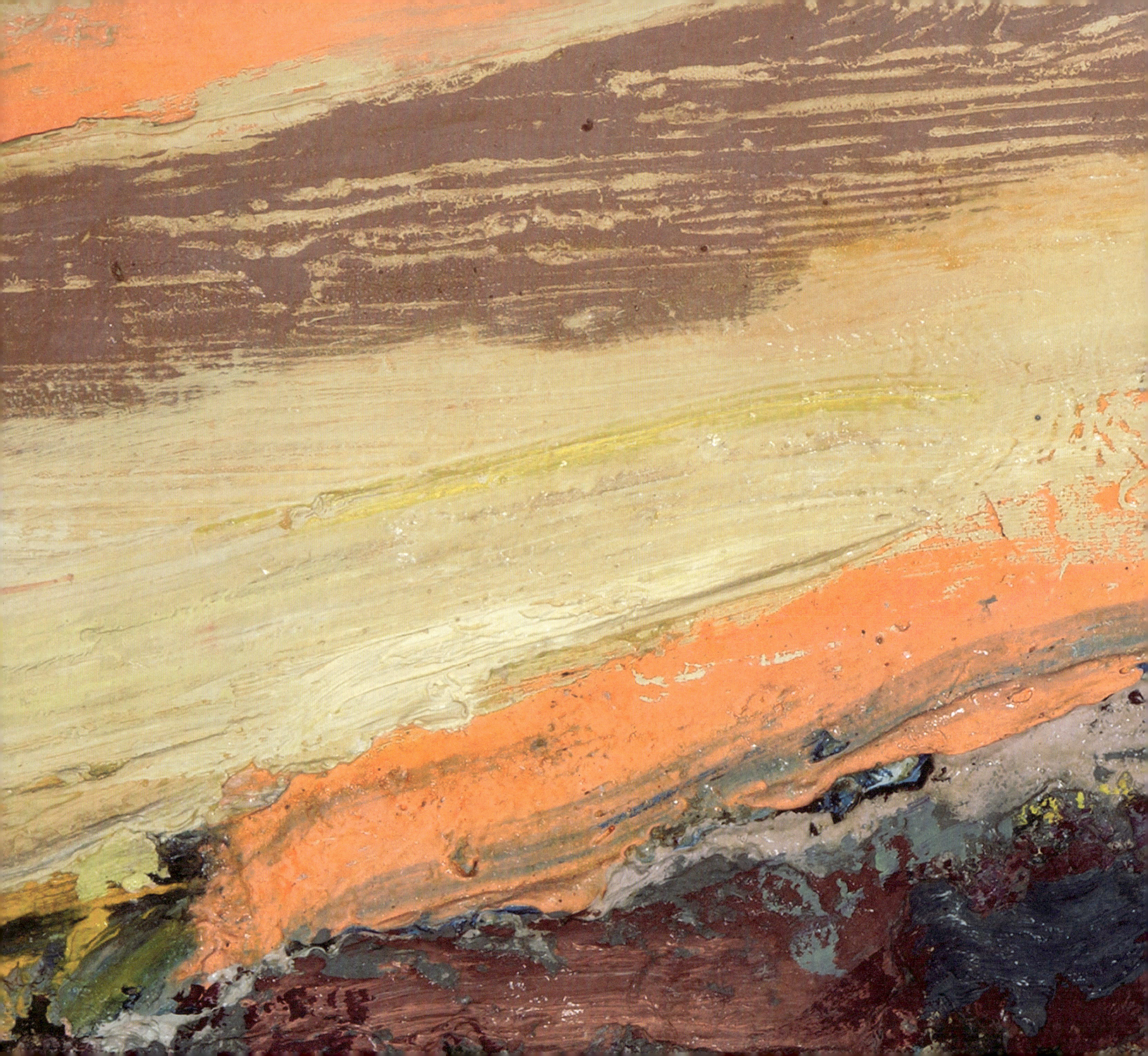